Byzantium

Also by this Author

The Holy Grail
St George

Byzantium

GILES MORGAN

CHARTWELL
BOOKS, INC.

This edition published in 2007 by
CHARTWELL BOOKS, INC.
A division of BOOK SALES, INC.
114 Northfield Avenue
Edison, New Jersey 08837
USA

A CIP catalogue record for this book is available from the Library of Congress.

ISBN 10: 0-7858-2290-9
ISBN 13: 978-0-7858-2290-5

2 4 6 8 10 9 7 5 3 1

Typeset by Avocet Typeset, Chilton, Aylesbury, Bucks, United Kingdom

Printed in UK by J. H. Haynes & Co. Ltd., Sparkford

For Gareth and Agnes

Contents

Byzantium

Introduction

In 312 AD, Constantine the Great saw a shining cross of light in the sky.

This is the legend that has become attached to the Roman Emperor who is today widely seen as having played a crucial role in the transmission of Christianity to the West. Constantine is often credited with having made two important and interlinked decisions that were to play a major part in the shaping of modern Europe. The first was his toleration, and subsequent adoption, of Christianity. The second was the relocation of the capital of the Empire to the site of the ancient Greek city of Byzantium. The term 'Byzantine' derives from this city of Byzantium, founded in 667 BC by Greek colonists from Megara and named in honour of their leader Byzas.

Re-founded as 'Nova Roma' or New Rome in 330 AD, this new capital became better known as Constantinople or the 'city of Constantine'.

The Byzantine Empire grew out of the Eastern half of the Roman Empire and was to continue long after the Western Empire finally fell to Germanic tribes in 476 AD. Indeed, the Byzantine Empire would endure until as late as 1453 and the eventual fall of Constantinople to the

Ottoman Turks. Until comparatively recently historians and scholars tended to dismiss the achievements and innovations of the Byzantine Empire as being of a lesser magnitude than those of ancient Greece and Rome. But increasingly there has been a reassessment of this view and an acknowledgement of the unique nature of Byzantine culture and its role in linking the ancient world with the medieval period.

In recent years the development of Christianity and the role of Constantine the Great in that process has come under intense scrutiny, particularly in the wake of the popular success of Dan Brown's novel *The Da Vinci Code*. Constantine is generally perceived as the first Christian Emperor but controversy has surrounded the differing forms that Christianity took in a period of intense theological debate. The varying movements within the Church would lead ultimately to the convening of the Council of Nicaea in an attempt to ratify Christian belief.

It is interesting to note, however, that, even as Christianity became the state religion of the Empire, many pagan beliefs, stories and ideas from the classical world survived and, indeed, were incorporated into the new dominant religion. Grave goods and luxury items, produced in Byzantine territories from different time periods up until as late as the Middle Ages, depict pre-Christian themes and images and challenge the idea that Byzantine art was solely concerned with Christian content.

Arguably, the Emperor Justinian I was to have as much influence over the development of the Byzantine Empire as

Constantine since he extended the boundaries of its lands substantially, notably within Italy and North Africa. Justinian was also responsible for the building of the legendary domed church of Hagia Sophia in Constantinople. During his lifetime Constantinople would become one of the major cities of the ancient world.

However, the authority and power of the Byzantine Empire were to be seriously tested by the rise of Islam. Territories belonging to the Empire were lost and the city of Constantinople withstood sieges by Arab navies. The Byzantines displayed great resourcefulness and technological ingenuity during these trying times, developing an incendiary substance known as 'Greek Fire' which appears to have had similar properties to napalm. The secret formula for its creation was said to only be known to the Emperors of Byzantium. It proved particularly effective when propelled by pumps, often in battles at sea.

Conflicts emerged within Byzantine Christianity over the worship of icons and, in 726 AD, Emperor Leo III banned them throughout the Empire. However, in 843 AD, this decision was overturned. Tensions between the Eastern and Western Church would lead eventually to the Great Schism of 1054 when the Pope and the Patriarch of Constantinople excommunicated one another, paving the way for the entirely separate Catholic and Eastern Orthodox Churches that we know today.

The defeat of Byzantine forces at the Battle of Manzikert by the Seljuk Turks resulted in appeals to the West for aid and precipitated the First Crusade. However, Constantinople was itself overrun by Crusader forces in 1204 during the Fourth Crusade. The fall of Constantinople to the Ottoman Turks in 1453 was a major shock to many Western European countries and has subsequently come to be seen as marking the end of the medieval period.

The collapse of the Byzantine Empire is considered to have contributed greatly to the Renaissance. Many scholars had to flee Constantinople to the West, carrying unique knowledge and material with them. Constantinople had also served as an important city linking East and West on the Silk Road and its loss sparked attempts to open up new trade routes. Exploration by sea following the fall of the Byzantine Empire would, in time, lead to important new discoveries by Europeans. The development of Christianity and Islam has been strongly influenced by the Byzantine Empire and its major legacy today is arguably the survival of the Orthodox Church. The staggering scale of the Empire at its peak is illustrated by the buildings that remain from its rule in countries ranging from Macedonia to Northern Africa. The art and architecture produced by the Byzantines is distinctive and fascinating as is their often incredible, and sometimes overlooked, story.

The Reign of Constantine the Great

It could be argued that no single individual played a greater role in the establishment and development of the Byzantine Empire than Constantine the Great. Like the immense marble head carved in his likeness that has survived from the fourth century AD at the Capitoline Museum in Rome, with its huge eyes and air of terrible power, his presence seems to dominate modern perceptions of Byzantium. However, to understand and trace the story of the Byzantine Empire, it is necessary to look first at the state of the Roman Empire under the Emperor Diocletian who ruled from 284 AD until his voluntary and unprecedented abdication in 305 AD.

During his reign Diocletian had divided the Empire into two halves formed of Eastern and Western parts. He shared his power with a trusted friend from the Roman military called Maximian, making him ruler in the West in 286 AD. Diocletian ruled the Eastern half of the Empire and retained ultimate power for himself. The decision to divide the Empire was an attempt to achieve greater control of what had become a vast and sprawling concern, stretching from Hadrian's Wall in Northern England to territories in Egypt. Diocletian divided the power structure still further with the appointment of two junior Caesars to serve the Emperors. These actions also reflected the fact that the city of Rome itself was no longer ideally placed in geographical terms to govern and control such a huge multi-national Empire. Diocletian based himself and his court primarily in the city of Nicomedia whilst Maximian ruled his half of the Empire principally from Milan.

This system of government was known as the Tetrachy. Apart from his structural changes, Diocletian is today most infamously remembered for his persecution of Christians throughout the Empire whom he saw as a pernicious, disruptive and divisive influence within Roman society. When Diocletian abdicated, weary with the pressures of power, he forced his reluctant co-emperor to do likewise and their two junior Caesars were declared 'Augusti' in their stead. Constantius Chlorus, nicknamed 'The Pale', took over the Western Empire whilst Galerius, a soldier with a vicious and formidable reputation, became Emperor in the East. Constantius Chlorus was the father of Constantine the Great and, following an impressive and successful career as a general in the Roman Army, he had been given the task of subduing unrest in the unruly province of Britain. Constantine's mother Helena is thought to have been the daughter of an innkeeper from Bithynia. Although historians generally concur that Constantius and Helena were at one time married, Helena was to be set aside in favour of a more prestigious and politically motivated marriage which Constantius made with Theodora, the adopted stepdaughter of the Emperor Maximian.

It is known that Constantine was born on 27 February but the exact year of his birth is not know for certain. It is thought to have been around 274 AD in a Roman province called Dacia. The town of his birth, Naissus, is known today as Nis in the former Republic of Yugoslavia. Although little is known about the origins of Constantine's parents, it seems that Constantius was an example of an increasing trend of the time for individuals to gain success within the Empire on the basis of merit and ability rather than simply high birth and attachment to one of the old families of the city of Rome. Diocletian himself was not from a Roman background but as an efficient and often ruthless soldier and leader he had gained power and approval within the Roman army.

Constantine spent his early life attached to the court of Diocletian at Nicomedia. Although this would have provided Constantine with an opportunity to serve and impress within the Emperor's court, it is likely that Diocletian kept him close as a potential bargaining tool should his father Constantius ever displease him or, indeed, openly rebel.

When Diocletian and Maximian did step down from power and Constantius and Galerius became Emperors, conflict almost immediately arose as to who was to take their place as Eastern and Western Caesars. Through the murky political machinations of the time Constantine was selected and left the court at Nicomedia in some haste to join his father's army in Gaul. There is every chance that, if he had remained, he would have been assassinated in order to prevent his coming to power.

When Constantine joined his father's army it was setting out on a military campaign against the Pictish tribes in Northern Britain. They succeeded in suppressing the marauding and aggressive Picts who had been wreaking havoc in Roman-controlled England and drove them back beyond the boundaries of Hadrian's Wall. However, soon after this success, Constantius became ill and he died suddenly at York on 25 July 306 AD. Constantine, who seems to have rapidly gained the respect and admiration of his father's troops during this campaign, was then acclaimed Augustus and 'raised to the purple'.

However, events were to run far less smoothly when the Eastern Emperor Galerius was informed of Constantine's acclamation by his troops. He refused to recognise Constantine as Western Emperor, viewing him as a rebellious upstart, and would accept him only as a Caesar and therefore junior to him in rank. In the short term Constantine was prepared to accept the situation and ruled in Britain and Gaul for a period of five years. Upon the death of Galerius in 311 AD, a power vacuum was created and rivalry between the Caesars came to a head. In the meantime the former Emperor Maximian, who had abdicated with Diocletian, had come back to power in Italy, supported by his son Maxentius. It is thought that Constantine may well have been involved in the later death of Maximian who had tried to make the legions of Gaul overthrow the younger man. Rivalry and mutual dislike was, therefore, particularly intense between Constantine and Maxentius and soon escalated into open war when Maxentius publicly accused Constantine of the murder of his father. Constantine is said to have raised an army of around 98,000 troops and marched on Italy. He successfully took a series of cities in Northern Italy and advanced inexorably on Rome to confront Maxentius.

The Battle of Milvian Bridge

The subsequent meeting of the two armies at the Battle of the Milvian Bridge on 28 October 312 AD has come to be seen as one of the defining moments in the life of Constantine with colossal implications for the future of European history. According to popular legend, Constantine is said to have undergone a profound and mystical religious experience either before or actually during the battle, one that could be compared to Paul's experience on the road to Damascus. Accounts of Constantine's vision vary and have subsequently proven to be an extremely popular and effective piece of pro-Christian propaganda. In his *Life of Constantine* (*De Vita Constantini, I*) the historian Eusebius of Caesarea tells how the Emperor described the experience to him:

…a most marvellous sign appeared to him from heaven… He said that about midday, when the sun was beginning to decline, he saw with his own eyes the trophy of a cross of light in the heavens, above the sun, and bearing the inscription 'Conquer by This'. At this sight he himself was struck with amazement, and his whole army also.

(quoted in John Julius Norwich,
Byzantium: The Early Years, p. 39).

Similarly the historian Socrates, who wrote his account in the fifth century, states that:

... at about that time of day when the sun, having passed the meridian, began to decline towards the West, he saw a pillar of light in the form of a cross which was inscribed 'in this conquer'. The appearance of the sign struck him with amazement, and doubting his own eyes, he asked those around him if they could see what he did, and as they unanimously declared that they could, the emperor's mind was strengthened by this divine and miraculous apparition.

(quoted in John Holland Smith,
Constantine the Great, p. 102).

Socrates further explains that Christ himself appeared to Constantine in a dream the next night and commanded him to make a standard in the shape of a cross and to carry it into battle. If he did so, he would be assured of victory.

However, the first text to record the alleged mystical events around the Battle of Milvian Bridge was produced by a writer called Lactantius who actually knew Constantine and his family. Writing within a relatively short period after the battle, he describes the sleeping

Constantine being directed in the course of a dream to order his troops to display the *chi rho* symbol. Constructed of the first two Greek letters of the name of Christ, this was a popular and well-known cipher for early Christians and can still be found in Christian contexts today. Historians now think that it is most likely that it was this symbol that Constantine utilised during the battle and that the vision of the cross was an elaboration which other contemporary accounts do not mention. It does seem, however, as if the Emperor did have some kind of experience that was meaningful to him and which he took to be of a divine origin and which greatly encouraged him before the battle took place.

When the two armies did meet it is thought that Constantine was leading the smaller of the two forces and yet he succeeded in forcing the troops of Maxentius into a disorderly retreat. The battle took place several miles from the city of Rome, near to the river Tiber and, in the melee, the army of Maxentius was pushed back to the Milvian Bridge, which was made of stone and fairly narrow. Knowing that it was possible that his troops might have to withdraw and would struggle to cross this bridge, Maxentius had ordered that a pontoon bridge be constructed next to it. Unfortunately, in the panic of retreat, the pontoon bridge was disassembled whilst men were still crossing it and it collapsed under their collective weight.

Many were drowned, including Maxentius himself, whilst the remaining men, who rushed to cross the stone bridge, became trapped and crushed by sheer weight of numbers. The army of Constantine emerged victorious, thus seeming to confirm the mystical dream or intuition of the Emperor.

The Edict of Milan

Following his victory at the Milvian Bridge and his acceptance by the Roman Senate as the Western Emperor, Constantine met with the Eastern Emperor Licinius in the city of Milan in early 313 AD. The subsequent talks between the two Emperors are best remembered today for producing the Edict of Milan which promised that there would be a new climate of religious tolerance and the cessation of persecution of individuals based on their beliefs. The edict was aimed particularly at protecting the Christians who had suffered greatly, particularly during the bloody and violent persecutions instituted by the Emperor Diocletian.

However, although Constantine was to legislate in favour of the Christians and had come to align himself with their cause, there is still considerable debate as to the extent to which he himself had embraced their religious beliefs. Clearly the events of the Battle of Milvian Bridge appear to show Constantine appealing to the Christian god for aid but a closer examination of what is known of the Emperor's religious beliefs during this period reveals a more complex spiritual identity. Constantine had in fact been variously a devotee of the cult of Apollo, of Mithras and of Sol Invictus or the 'Unconquered Sun'. Coins from the early part of his reign as Western Emperor depict Sol Invictus and it has been argued that, like his own father Constantius, he was increasingly becoming interested and moving towards the idea of a single supreme deity. Interestingly, however (and, arguably, entirely in keeping with attitudes of the time), Constantine seems to have felt reasonably comfortable with, and open to, the concept of this supreme deity taking more than one form or assuming more than one identity. It must also be remembered that it would have been politically unwise of Constantine to commit fully and publicly to the Christian cause and so upset the long-standing traditions of polytheistic worship in the Roman Empire.

Following his victory at the Milvian Bridge he seems to have been careful to remain reasonably ambiguous about his own religious beliefs, even adopting the tactic of appearing to be above such concerns. One particular inscription of the time, drafted by the senate and presumably approved by the Emperor, survives on the triumphal Arch of Constantine and describes him as being 'Instinct With Divinity'. Tellingly, it omits to say which divinity, suggesting a certain caution and wariness about proclaiming where exactly his convictions might lie. It is also possible that Constantine had not himself fully decided and, as we have seen, the worship and recognition of more than one God was perfectly normal for the time.

Following Constantine's acceptance as Western Emperor relations with his Eastern counterpart Licinius soon deteriorated. Tensions between the two finally resulted in war in 323 AD with Constantine emerging as the victor. At first Constantine showed clemency, exiling Licinius to

Thessalonica, but within months he had him executed, perhaps sensing that, whilst he lived, he represented a threat to his authority.

The Arian Heresy

Perhaps the single greatest threat to the unity of the early Christian Church was the emergence and development of the heresy often known as Arianism. It was a Christian theology that took its name from a presbyter of Alexandria named Arius. He had been a pupil of Lucian of Antioch and his teachings were to send shockwaves through the hierarchy of the early Church. Arius was born in 256 AD and it is thought he was of Berber or possibly Libyan ancestry. He was made presbyter of Alexandria in 313 AD. The views of Arius were not, in fact, new or unique but, through his personal charisma and magnetism, they achieved great popularity throughout the Christian world. At the centre of his heretical teachings was the nature of Christ and his relationship to God. It must be remembered that what is known of Arius' teachings has survived largely in the writings and texts of those who were opposed to him. Arius argued that Christ was not of the same substance as God and that he was not eternal and had, in fact, been a creation of God. If God had created the son then there necessarily must have been a time when the son had not existed and therefore must be lesser than God and not co-eternal with him. The followers of St Alexander of Alexandria disputed this, saying that the Son and the Father were of the same substance and were co-eternal. St Alexander and his supporters were known as homoousians. A third theological position contested that Christ and God were of a 'similar' substance and adherents of this Christological viewpoint were called homoiousians. By arguing that Christ was not equal to God, Arius effectively questioned the Holy Trinity and contested the divinity of Christ. In Arius' view, Jesus had been created by God to perform a particular function on earth, the salvation of humanity, but was himself human in nature. His theology was hugely popular but, by 320 AD, Arius had been excommunicated for his heretical beliefs.

The Council of Nicaea

In response to the discord and disharmony that Arianism had created within the Church, in 323 AD Constantine sent an emissary, Bishop Hosius of Cordova, on a mission to Egypt to try and resolve a dispute which, from the Emperor's point of view, threatened the unity and stability of the Empire. Hosius had been Constantine's own personal advisor on Christianity but he was unable to resolve the issue.

A further attempt the following year also met with failure and Constantine ultimately took the decision to convene a universal church council to reach a final and decisive conclusion on the matter. This council began on 20 May 325 AD and continued until 19 June and was held at Nicaea, a place chosen as the meeting point because it was reachable without too much difficulty by all the delegates, particularly those at the centre of the dispute in the East. Estimates vary as to how many attended the council at the imperial palace in Nicaea. The chronicler Eusebius of Caesarea claims 270 bishops but it is thought, on the basis of other contemporary accounts, that a figure of between 300 and 318 is more likely. Most of these bishops had travelled from the East. Each bishop was also allowed to bring two presbyters and three deacons. Most significantly, Constantine himself attended the council, an action that drew the state and the Church together in a manner that would come to define the history of the Byzantine Empire. The council decided that the Father and the Son were co-substantial or of one substance, a rejection of Arian beliefs.

In recent years the findings and the events of the Council of Nicaea have been called into question, most notably in Dan Brown's best-selling *The Da Vinci Code*. In Brown's version of events, a character named Leigh Teabing states that until the Council of Nicaea, 'Jesus was viewed by his followers as a mortal prophet... a great and powerful man, but a man nonetheless' (Dan Brown, *The Da Vinci Code*, p.240).

Moreover, Teabing goes on to say that, 'Jesus' establishment as the "Son of God" was officially proposed and voted on by the Council of Nicaea' and makes the claim that it was, 'A relatively close vote at that', (Dan Brown, *The Da Vinci Code*, p.241). In fact, only two of those present refused to sign the statement of belief that is known as the Nicene Creed. The teachings of Arius were declared to be heretical and condemned and he himself was sent into exile. Whilst there may be truth in the idea that Constantine wanted to secure peace in the Church and throughout his Empire, the claim that he 'invented' the divinity of Christ for his own political ends is not supported by most historians. In a letter to Arius and Alexander of 324 AD the Emperor wrote:

> Having enquired faithfully into the origin and foundation of your differences, I find their cause to be of a truly insignificant nature, and quite unworthy of such fierce contention.
>
> (quoted in John Julius Norwich, *Byzantium: The Early Years*, p.53).

The Byzantine historian John Julius Norwich tellingly writes that, 'It is plain from Constantine's letter to the two chief disputants that the doctrinal point at issue interested him not at all', (John Julius Norwich, *Byzantium: The Early Years*, p.55).

The aims of the council had been to settle the question of Arianism but also to resolve other issues. Most famously, the question of when Easter should be celebrated was discussed. In the East, churches followed the Jewish calendar because Christ had been crucified during the feast of Passover but, in the West and in Alexandria, it took place on the first Sunday following the first full moon after the vernal equinox. It was decided that the church at Alexandria would calculate the date of Easter each year.

They would then communicate this information to the Holy See of Rome which, in turn, would pass it on to the wider Church. On this point Constantine is known to have had considerable influence. He was violently opposed to the Christian Church following the Jewish calendar and personally was strongly anti-Semitic.

However, although the Council of Nicaea appeared to have been a major success for Constantine in that Arianism had been anathematised, the controversy failed to go away. Surprisingly, given the findings of the Council of Nicaea, the supporters of Arius continued to propagate his beliefs and were active in attempting to have him recalled from exile. Perhaps the greatest surprise is that the Emperor himself was swayed by the arguments of Arius and that his own family, including his sister and mother, were sympathetic to his cause. By 327 AD the decision to keep Arius in exile had been overturned by Constantine and he had granted him a personal audience.

Far from being resolved, it seemed that Arianism would continue to pose a threat to the unity of the early Church.

Constantinople

Having established his supreme authority throughout the Roman Empire, Constantine took the decision to establish a new capital on the site of the ancient city of Byzantium. As with so many aspects of the Emperor's life, many myths and legends have sprung up about the circumstances surrounding this momentous decision and once again God himself is supposed to have influenced Constantine in his choice. According to the British chronicler William of Malmesbury, the Emperor had a mysterious dream in which he saw an old woman transform magically into a young and beautiful one. In a subsequent dream, the deceased Pope Sylvester visited Constantine and informed him that the woman he had seen represented the city of Byzantium and that the Emperor was to rejuvenate and renew it. Most famously Constantine is said to have personally laid out the plan for the walls of Constantinople by pacing out their dimensions and demarcating them with the point of his spear. Legend tells that an observer showed surprise at the scale of the city limits that the Emperor was planning and that he replied that he would carry on until 'he who walks ahead of me bids me stop'. Once again there is an ambiguity about this statement – the divinity or otherwise to which he refers is not named.

However, it is likely that Constantine was equally swayed by far more pressing and practical concerns in his decision to found a new capital city for the Empire.

During the fourth century, the Eastern territories of the empire had become more economically productive than the West and Italy itself had experienced increasing problems with illness and population shrinkage. Importantly, as has been mentioned before, Rome itself was no longer strategically placed to defend such a huge concern. The greatest military threats were similarly concentrated in the East, particularly near the lower Danube. The sprawling Sassanian Empire of the Persians had conquered Armenia, which had previously belonged to the Romans, and posed the single greatest danger to Constantine. Although a peace treaty had been agreed between the Emperor Galerius and King Narses, this was due to expire and a resumption of hostilities was expected.

It was originally intended that Byzantium should be known as 'Nova Roma' or 'New Rome' and this title was carved on a number of monuments in the city. However, it rapidly became better known as Constantinople, meaning the 'city of Constantine'. It is thought that the Emperor took the decision to re-site the capital in around 324 AD. The consecration of the city took place on 4 November 328 AD and combined both Christian and decidedly pagan elements. Once again, Constantine seemed to feel entirely comfortable with invoking the blessing and protection of a number of differing divinities. The city was formally dedicated on Monday 11 May 330 AD, an event which was planned to coincide with the Emperor's own silver jubilee celebrations. It is said that many of the cities of the ancient world were stripped of their statues and monuments and that these were transferred to Constantinople, further enhancing its own status within the Empire and its fame beyond its own borders. Near the old acropolis of Byzantium, Constantine ordered the building of the 'Milion', the first milestone. A construction of arches forming a square, this was surmounted by the True Cross, a sacred relic that purported to be the actual cross that Christ was crucified upon and said to have been discovered by Constantine's mother Helena on a pilgrimage to

Jerusalem. It was intended to serve as the centre of the Empire and all distances were calculated from it.

Athanasius

Despite the success of the foundation of Constantinople and the unification of the Empire under Constantine, Arianism had continued to sow the seeds of discord and divide the early Church. Perhaps the greatest opponent of Arius and his followers to emerge at this time was Athanasius of Alexandria. He had been a deacon in the church of Alexandria when Arius had first achieved prominence with his views and later accompanied Alexander, Bishop of Alexandria to the Council of Nicaea.

Both men had vehemently opposed Arius and Athanasius was to succeed Alexander as Bishop of Alexandria in 328 AD. When Constantine rescinded the exile of Arius, he wrote to Bishop Alexander to recommend his re-instatement to the Church on the basis that Arius, although his personal interpretation of it may have been open to question, had accepted the Nicene Creed.

Alexander refused to do so and so, in his turn, did Athanasius. Conflict between the opposing factions eventually led to Constantine sending Athanasius into exile in Trier (Tyre). However, attempts to restore Arius in Alexandria proved extremely unpopular and led to rioting in the city. In the wake of these troubles, Constantine summoned Arius to Constantinople in 336 AD to discuss once again the latter's beliefs.

At this point, fate seemed to intervene in the proceedings when Arius, who was walking through the city of Constantinople with a crowd of his followers, was suddenly overcome with an urge to evacuate his bowels. On being directed to a private place behind the Forum of Constantine, the unfortunate Arius is said to have haemorrhaged to death whilst relieving himself. The accounts that survive of this grisly incident are supplied mainly by the opponents of Arius and yet most sources seem in agreement that it did indeed take place. These sources maintain that it was divine retribution although it may be that Arius had, in fact, been murdered by his enemies. His death may have lessened the conflict but dissent in the Church was to continue in the following centuries. Athanasius is revered today in the Catholic and Eastern Orthodox Church and is often seen as the first to identify the works that make up the New Testament.

The Death of Constantine

In 337 AD Constantine became ill and instructed that his tomb be prepared in the Church of the Holy Apostles at Constantinople. As his health worsened Constantine finally took the decision to be baptised and summoned Bishop Eusebius of Nicomedia to perform the ceremony. Controversy has raged as to why he waited until he was on his deathbed to be baptised but it seems likely that he regarded the ritual as a final and dramatic absolution of all his sins and so waited until his life was nearly at an end.

Constantine had often referred to himself as the 'Equal of the Apostles' and instructed that twelve sarcophagi be set upright in the church, each one representing the original followers of Christ, and that his own should be set in the middle of them. He intended that his own tomb should be worshipped alongside the Holy Apostles and it seems probable that he saw himself not simply as their equal, but in fact their superior. Constantine died on the 22 May 337 AD and, several months later, amidst great pomp and ceremony, his body was placed in its tomb in the Church of the Holy Apostles.

The Roman Empire in Crisis

Julian the Apostate

The death of Constantine, although commemorated solemnly and reverently, was followed by a period of turmoil and some surprising reversals in the Empire.

In the immediate aftermath of his funeral his sons Constantine II, Constantius II and Constans were proclaimed as the new Augusti. However, the shift of power was accompanied by a series of violent intrigues within the ruling family as individuals began to attempt to secure their hold on power. Constantius in particular took the opportunity to eliminate potential rivals and had all his half-brothers killed on dubious charges of treachery against his father. Those close to or related to the unfortunate victims were similarly caught up in a wave of violent reprisals. These events conveniently cleared the way for the three full brothers, Constantine, Constantius and Constans, to divide the Empire between themselves without threat of challenge or rivalry.

They essentially retained the territories that they had ruled as Caesars under Constantine. Constantine II governed the Western regions, Gaul, Spain and Britain, whilst Constantius held the Eastern countries and Constans had responsibility for Africa, Italy and much of central Europe. It would seem, then, that each brother had been well rewarded and that each had achieved power on a vast and imposing scale. But in the age-old tradition of imperial infighting it was not long before conflict arose between them as each sought to assert his ultimate authority. Constantine II was killed by his brother Constans after invading Italy. However, Constans was himself then overthrown and murdered by an outsider from Britain called Magnentius. The surviving brother Constantius put down this insurrection and became sole ruler of the Empire.

The scale and problems of governing such a vast Empire led Constantius to choose a new co-ruler in 355 AD. He selected his cousin Julian for this role, a responsibility that the younger man was apparently (and perhaps understandably) reluctant at first to take. Julian had been born in the city of Constantinople in 331 AD, the son of Constantine the Great's half-brother, Julius Constantius. His mother was called Basilina and she was his father's second wife. Unlike so many rulers of the period Julian did not come from a military background but was a scholar and an intellectual who had studied at some of the best schools of the ancient world. He was not overly ambitious and appears not to have constituted any kind of threat to Constantius, which is, perhaps, precisely why he was chosen.

Although Julian was chosen as Constantius' co-ruler

because he was co-operative and, to a certain extent, malleable, he was, in another important respect, something of a rebel. Privately Julian was to abandon Christianity and revert to the pagan religions of the ancient world. His personal opinions on spirituality were initially kept to himself but they would assume greater importance in the longer term. His decision to abandon Christianity was to earn him the title of Julian the Apostate, a title bestowed on him by Christian writers and critics.

Julian was made Caesar of the West on 6 November 355 AD at Milan and was subsequently dispatched to Gaul. Before beginning his duties in Gaul he was married to Helena, the sister of Constantius II. Although he was without previous military experience and was thought by many to be an unlikely candidate for his new role, Julian proved successful, winning back Cologne and other territories from the Franks in 356 AD. Perhaps his greatest triumph at this time was the defeat of the Franks at a battle near Strasbourg where, commanding a force of 13,000 soldiers, he triumphed over a Frankish force estimated to be 30,000 strong. In these campaigns, Julian successfully re-imposed Roman control in areas that had been previously lost to the Empire in the West, proving himself to be a formidable and capable Caesar.

However, Constantius II faced a far greater threat when, in 359 AD, Shapur, King of Persia, demanded that he cede the Roman territories of Mesopotamia and Armenia or face an invasion. Faced with the prospect of war with the powerful Persian king, Constantius turned to Julian for aid and called on him to send reinforcements amounting to over half of Julian's own forces in Gaul. The request was met with anger and outrage amongst the troops, many of whom had been promised that they would be allowed to stay in Gaul. They were unwilling to risk either dying on campaign in the East or leaving their possessions and families unprotected in the West. In the unrest that followed Julian urged his legionaries to comply with the command of Constantius and there is no evidence to suggest that he was anything other than loyal to the Eastern Emperor. But Julian appears to have been swept along by events as his troops defied the orders of Constantius and instead acclaimed Julian Emperor in Paris, effectively forcing him into opposition against his cousin. Although Julian attempted to resolve matters peacefully with Constantius, some kind of confrontation between the two seemed almost inevitable. However, shortly after Constantius had taken the decision, albeit reluctant, to confront Julian with an army, he was over-come by a mysterious illness and died whilst returning to Constantinople from Syria. Julian was immediately and unanimously declared sole Emperor.

Once accepted as supreme ruler Julian undertook a number of changes and reforms that were to characterise and define his reign. Interestingly, he took the decision to greatly reduce the numbers of people employed in the court at Constantinople. These had grown to extravagant and excessive numbers. In this and in other instances, Julian appears to have been a man with little interest in hedonistic pursuits or material possessions and to have been chiefly preoccupied by philosophy and religion.

Indeed, Julian is best remembered today for reversing many of the pro-Christian initiatives of the Christian Emperors who followed Constantine. However, unlike many of his pagan predecessors, Julian did not undertake a programme of persecution against Christians. Instead, he attempted to sideline them and their significance through a series of social and legal reforms. Julian, it is thought, believed that Christianity was responsible for undermining the power of the Empire and sapping its vitality and strength. He legalised all religions, encouraged polytheism and allowed the old temples to be occupied and used again. By declaring a state of religious toleration Julian may well have been attempting to allow suppressed forms of Christianity, such as Arianism, to thrive and create greater division within the unity of the Church. Some authorities of the time also claim that Julian believed that he was the reincarnation of Alexander the Great.

During many of the key moments of his life and career he had looked to the gods for divine guidance and portents and, indeed, he viewed the sudden death of Constantius as evidence that he was destined to rule. When the temple of Apollo at Daphne was burnt down on 26 October 362 AD, as Julian was readying himself for a war against Persia, it was believed that Christians were responsible. In retaliation the principal church of Antioch was closed and its gold plate was seized.

On 5 March 363 AD, Julian led his army of about

90,000 men out of Antioch to war against the Persian Empire. Whilst Constantius had been Emperor in the East, the Persian King, Shapur II, had conquered a number of key cities in the East that had previously been under Roman rule and now he posed a dangerous threat to Roman territories. Julian's army marched east into what is now Iraq, winning a number of minor engagements along the way, until they reached the Persian capital city of Ctesiphon. The ruins of Ctesiphon are located twenty miles away from the city of Baghdad on the eastern side of the river Tigris. Julian's forces were confronted with a Persian army which had taken up its positions in front of the city walls. Despite facing the difficulty of crossing the Tigris before any fighting could even begin, the Roman army succeeded, after some strong resistance, in over-whelming the Persians.

However, jubilation at the victory was short-lived when Julian's forces were unable to take the city itself. The Emperor now faced several problems. The main Persian army was advancing rapidly to Ctesiphon and the Roman army was running out of supplies. Even so, Julian wanted to push further into Persian territory but was persuaded against doing so. The decision to retreat was taken and, as they did so, the Roman forces were hounded by Persian troops. On 26 June 363 AD, Persian forces launched a fierce attack against Julian's soldiers that was successfully repulsed, but not before the Emperor himself was fatally wounded by a spear that struck him in his lower intestines. Courageously, but rashly, Julian had rushed into battle with his men without putting on his armour and he had paid the ultimate price for his impetuosity. He died of his injury later that day. In the years following his death, a myth grew that Julian's last words after his fatal wounding had been, 'Vicisti, Galileae' which translates as 'Thou hast conquered, Galilean'. This is more likely to be a subsequent Christian invention aimed at showing how the Emperor had suffered divine retribution for his pagan beliefs and opposition to the Christian Church. It was even said that the Eastern Orthodox Saint Mercurius, acting as the weapon of God, had struck the fatal blow to the Emperor.

Julian's untimely and, arguably, needless death left both the Eastern Empire and, more immediately, the Eastern army leaderless and in a precarious and dangerous position. Still deep within enemy territory, the army was forced to appoint a new Emperor, which they did the next day. What happened seems confused. The commander of the Imperial Guard, a man named Jovian, was nominated by some of his fellow soldiers. He appears not to have been a particularly popular choice but, in the emotionally charged atmosphere, the majority apparently misheard those who took up the cry of his name and thought that the name of the old Emperor was being shouted. Jovian seems to have been elected by the army, in effect, because they believed that Julian was still alive. In the immediate aftermath of Jovian's succession his priority was to lead the army out of danger and an orderly but urgent retreat took place. The enemy troops continued to hound them nonetheless and, ultimately, Jovian was forced to accept a very one-sided agreement with King Shapur. In return for their safe passage Jovian agreed to relinquish control of lands bordering the Persian Empire and a number of significant defensive positions. Armenia would also be left open to Persian invasion under Shapur's terms.

Jovian led the army away from what had become a costly and embarrassing disaster but, as soon as he arrived in the city of Antioch, he launched a series of religious edicts that were pro-Christian in nature. He was himself a committed Christian who accepted the Nicene Creed over Arianism and this was reflected in his religious policies. However, Jovian's reign was to be short-lived. He died in early 364 AD, thought to have been accidentally overcome by fumes as he slept one night.

Emperor Valens

Following the death of the Emperor Jovian, a successor was sought from within the military. A man named Valentinian was elected and proclaimed as Emperor on 26 February 364 AD. He inherited an Empire which faced many threats to its borders and to its security and he decided to select a co-ruler to share the formidable and challenging task of ruling it. Valentinian made his own brother Valens co-Emperor. Valentinian became Western Emperor whilst Valens was given the Eastern half of the Empire. When Valentinian died in 375 AD he was succeeded by his own son, Gratian.

During Valens' reign as Emperor the Gothic tribes of Northern Europe came under attack from the Huns who originated in Mongolia. Unable to defend themselves against the ferocity of the Huns, in 376 AD the Gothic tribes asked that Valens allow them to move and create settlements within the boundaries of the Empire in Thrace.

Valens agreed to this on the basis that they would become allies of the Emperor and he instructed the provincial powers to help them settle and become part of the Empire.

However, the local authorities did just the opposite and treated the Goths unfairly and cruelly. A critical error of judgement, this failure to comply with the orders of Valens led to a widespread revolt amongst the Gothic tribes. There followed two years of fighting between the Goths and the forces of the Empire without either side gaining the upper hand. In the West the Emperor Gratian achieved an important victory over the Alemanni tribe near the river Rhine in 378 AD. Valens, eager for success against the Goths in the East, set out with the army to confront what he believed was a small Gothic force near Adrianople in what is today Northern Turkey, not far from Constantinople itself.

The Battle of Adrianople

The Battle of Adrianople took place on 9 August 378 AD and is widely viewed today as having been one of the worst defeats in Roman history. Not since the Battle of Cannae, six hundred years earlier, when the Carthaginian general Hannibal had overcome the combined forces of eight legions, had so many Roman soldiers been killed in a single day. The Emperor, perhaps urged by some of his advisors, took the decision to confront the combined Gothic forces without waiting for the forces of the Western Emperor Gratian to arrive. Valens had received reports that the barbarian forces did not exceed 10,000 men and he was eager to take the credit for an impressive victory. Before setting out for the battle, Valens weakened his own forces by leaving soldiers to guard his baggage and treasures at the city of Hadrianopolis (Adrianople).

The Roman army marched eight miles to meet the Gothic army in blistering heat and across rough terrain. They found the Gothic troops had arranged their wagons in a circle with their families and goods inside it. Initially the Goths, led by a warrior named Fritigern, had sent ambassadors to Valens to ask for peace but this was largely a delaying tactic because they were waiting for the arrival of their cavalry. The Gothic forces had burnt the surrounding fields and the resulting smoke added to the discomfort of the tired and thirsty Roman troops. A group of Roman archers, led by a man named Bacurius from Iberia, attacked the Goths without permission and were then forced to flee. The resultant confusion gave the Gothic cavalry enough time to reach their comrades. With the arrival of the Gothic cavalry, the Roman cavalry panicked and fled, leaving the infantry undefended. Surrounded by enemy cavalry, forced into a close formation and unable to manoeuvre or escape, the Roman troops were massacred.

As much as two thirds of the Roman army was destroyed during the battle including many important officers, administrators and officials. According to the Roman historian Ammianus Marcellinus (330–395AD) some reports stated that the Emperor received a mortal wound from an arrow and died without his body ever being recovered. Other reports maintained that he managed to escape the field of battle after being hit by an arrow and was taken to a small house or cabin by soldiers and court eunuchs. They were attempting to dress his wounds when the cabin was surrounded by enemy troops. They barred the doors and windows to the besiegers who were unaware of the identity of its occupants. The Gothic soldiers reacted to being shot at with arrows from its roof by setting fire to the building. All the defenders were said to have been burnt alive, including the Emperor himself, apart from one person who leapt from the windows and told them what had happened. Marcellinus observed that even this inglorious end was preferable to the humiliation of being taken prisoner by the enemy.

The death of Valens and the defeat of the imperial army, together with the loss of so many important individuals, left the Western Roman Emperor Gratian in a state of crisis. The Battle of Adrianople changed the course of the history of warfare. Until that point the Roman Infantry had been considered the ultimate military force but the success of the Gothic cavalry forced the Empire to abandon this long-held belief. In subsequent centuries the cavalry became the most important and decisive component of the Roman army.

Theodosius I

In the aftermath of the appalling defeat of the imperial army at the Battle of Adrianople, the Emperor Gratian found himself increasingly preoccupied with problems in the Western Empire. For help in the East, he turned to a former military commander from Spain called Theodosius, making him co-Augustus in 379 AD.

Theodosius was the son of a military figure who had put down an uprising in Britain in 368 AD, Theodosius the Elder. However, his father had been executed by the Emperor Valens in 376 AD for reasons which are unclear and the younger Theodosius had himself retired from service at around the same time. It was from this premature retirement in Spain that he was now summoned. He proved very successful at reaching a solution with the renegade Gothic forces, making fresh treaties with their leaders in which they agreed to fight alongside the Emperor and became part of the Roman army. As reward for serving in the legions they were granted special privileges such as freedom from having to pay taxes. Many within the Empire felt concern over the growing importance and status of Goths within the Empire and anger at their sometimes superior rights but these measures of Theodosius achieved peace. When the Emperor Gratian was overthrown and later killed by a general who had been acclaimed Augustus in Britain, Theodosius supported his successor Valentinian II and helped to defeat the usurper Maximus.

During 387 AD Theodosius was faced with rioting in the city of Antioch because of a tax that he had levied on its people to raise money for the celebrations to mark his tenth anniversary in power, an event known as the deccenalia. Such was the unpopularity of the tax that many statues of the Emperor were smashed and Antioch was rocked by serious unrest. However, imperial punishment was swift and uncompromising and many citizens were killed by soldiers for their insurrectionary behaviour. The incident harmed the reputation of Theodosius who had hitherto been generally viewed as a fair and just Emperor. Worse was to follow when an angry mob killed the captain of the imperial garrison in the city of Thessalonica. The people of Thessalonica were angered by the behaviour of Gothic troops within the army and particularly their leader, a man named Botheric, who was serving as captain of the garrison. The news of this unfortunate civic unrest so angered Theodosius, who was in the city of Milan at the time, that he ordered those troops serving in Thessalonica to punish the people without mercy or pity. Bishop Ambrose of Milan attempted to persuade the Emperor against extreme action and, in fact, Theodosius did reconsider his commands. However, as soon as his initial decree reached Thessalonica, the troops stationed there, eager for revenge, attacked the people of the city whilst they were inside the hippodrome watching the games. They were trapped by the soldiers and it is said that as many as 7,000 people were slaughtered by them. This excessive and violent reprisal shocked many throughout the Empire and led to Bishop Ambrose personally withholding communion from Theodosius. The significance of these events and their aftermath is that for the first time a Christian figure claimed a greater authority than the Emperor himself. Bishop Ambrose informed Theodosius that he must pay a personal penance for his actions and the Emperor, who was overcome by remorse and guilt, agreed. Theodosius, dressed in sackcloth, had to seek the forgiveness of the Bishop at the Cathedral of Milan and admit to his sins.

Although Theodosius had helped support the Western Emperor Valentinian II against a pretender to the throne, his position was to prove far from assured. Valentinian had joined forces with Theodosius to overcome Maximus and, upon the successful accomplishment of this goal, they had jointly handed power to a general of Frankish origin called Arbogast. He was to rule in Gaul whilst Valentinian and Theodosius made a formal visit to Rome in 389 AD and attended to imperial business.

However, when Theodosius returned to Constantinople and Valentinian to Gaul in 391 AD, Arbogast refused to hand power back to the Western Emperor. War seemed inevitable but it was briefly averted by the sudden death of Valentinian. Arbogast manipulated the situation by appointing a puppet Emperor called Eugenius whom he intended to control from behind the scenes. Theodosius refused to acknowledge the authority of either and further division was created by Eugenius' policies of allowing pagan worship to resume in Rome. Theodosius marched on the rebels in 394 AD and the two forces engaged near Trieste at the battle of the Frigidus River. The significance of the battle for many at the time, apart from the assertion of the rule of Theodosius, was that it was fought in defence of the supremacy of the Christian faith. After some early difficulties, mercenary deserters from the rebel army bolstered the forces of Theodosius. The Eastern Emperor proved victorious and Eugenius was executed. Arbogast was forced into flight, despair and ultimately suicide. Valentinian II left no heir to his throne and Theodosius took the decision to appoint his eldest son Arcadius as Eastern Emperor. His youngest son Honorius was made Western Emperor. Shortly afterwards, Theodosius became seriously ill and died on 17 January 395 AD in the city of Milan.

Emperor Arcadius

When Arcadius was appointed as Eastern Emperor by his father Theodosius he was still only eighteen. His brother Honorius was even younger, aged only ten. In view of their tender years and inexperience, Theodosius appointed a relative by marriage named Stilicho, who had supported him loyally, to the position of *magister militum* in Italy. He was to assist both the young Emperors in their early years. Stilicho was not from a Roman background but was a

Vandal who had proved his worth in the imperial service, particularly at the Battle of the Frigidus. Arcadius, however, soon fell under the influence of a powerful and ambitious minister called Rufinus in Constantinople. Arcadius was to prove susceptible to influence and persuasion from more than one source and he appears also to have become dominated by the high-ranking eunuch Eutropius. When Rufinus attempted to arrange a marriage between his own daughter and Arcadius and thus gain greater power and influence over him, Eutropius engineered a match between the Emperor and a young woman of his own choosing. He picked a bride of Frankish origin called Eudoxia. They were married in 395 AD.

However, Arcadius was soon faced with a major uprising from the Goths under the leadership of Alaric who had fought alongside Theodosius at the Battle of the Frigidus. Alaric's army marched on Constantinople, which was particularly vulnerable at this point because many of the troops that Theodosius had led to the West had not yet returned. In the event, although the Goths sacked and plundered town and country, marching through what is now Macedonia, they did not attack Constantinople itself. Instead they retraced their steps back through Macedonia and into Greece. Terrified by these events, Arcadius instructed Stilicho in the West to send the army of the East back as soon as possible. Upon their return to Constantinople, under the command of a Goth called Gainas, the Emperor greeted the army in person. Rufinus, who had come to exert considerable power over Arcadius, was suddenly and unexpectedly murdered by some of the Gothic troops. It is unclear who had given orders for the killing but he clearly presented a threat to the ambitions of many close to Arcadius.

Gainas attempted to claim greater powers for himself and succeeded in tricking Arcadius into handing over the influential eunuch Eutropius in 399 AD in order to calm a potential Gothic rebellion. However, Gainas himself failed to gain greater powers and, after unsuccessful scheming, was forced to leave the city with his troops. After the death of Arcadius in 408 AD his son Theodosius II inherited the Eastern Empire.

In the West the political machinations of Stilicho and, in particular, his apparently ambivalent attitude to the renegade Goth Alaric finally led to his arrest and execution for treachery in 408 AD. Interestingly, Alaric, who had invaded Italy in 401 AD but was defeated and mysteriously released by Stilicho, seems not to have wanted to destroy the Empire. Ironically, he wanted a role within it and a permanent base and recognition for his fellow Goths. The refusal of the Western Emperor Honorius to come to terms with Alaric, who had proved he could be a formidable opponent, was ultimately to result in the Goth leader re-invading Italy in 408 AD after the execution of Stilicho. Without a strong military leader and in the incompetent hands of Honorius, the Western Empire had become dangerously vulnerable. However, Alaric still asked for terms even though he held the upper hand. Again, he was refused. Whilst Honorius remained within the relative safety of

Ravenna, Alaric finally besieged and captured Rome in 410 AD.

John Chrysostom

During the reign of the Emperor Arcadius one of the most influential, although divisive, figures within the Church and Byzantine culture was John Chrysostom who was appointed bishop of Constantinople in 398 AD. The name Chrysostom comes from the Greek word 'chrysostomos' and means 'golden mouthed'. Interestingly, Chrysostom had been reluctant to take the post of bishop of Constantinople because he was opposed to the wealth and privileges that went with the position. Indeed, he was outspoken in condemning excess and corruption within the Church in general and was well known for speaking on behalf of the poor. This made him an often unpopular figure with the wealthy and the powerful. He was outspoken in his views and not afraid to be controversial. This would seem to be the origin of the term 'golden mouthed' bestowed after his death.

He was particularly critical of the Empress Eudoxia who was known to have a string of lovers and to be lavish and extravagant in her lifestyle. His criticisms led to his banishment in 403 AD but he was quickly restored by Arcadius. However, his disputes with Eudoxia led to a further banishment and Chrysostom died in exile in Georgia in 407 AD. He had proved to be a figure who had enjoyed great popularity amongst the general populace in the East and he also

had papal support in the West but his condemnation of
Eudoxia was to lead to something of a rift between Rome
and Constantinople. Arcadius refused to accept the authority of Rome and there was a growing sense of division
between the two halves of the Church.

The Reign of Justinian

When the Eastern Emperor Arcadius died in 408 AD his son Theodosius II, who was only a boy of seven at the time, succeeded him. During his reign the fortifications of Constantinople were greatly enlarged and expanded and the city surrounded by defences named in his honour, the Theodosian Walls. The walls are sixty feet in height and around four miles in length. They enclosed the city from attack by land and were to prove incredibly effective, remaining unbreached for over a thousand years. They were built between 413 and 414 AD and the man truly responsible for their construction was the young emperor's guardian Anthemius who was Prefect of the city. The Theodosian Walls were to protect the city from the army of Attila the Hun in 447 AD. Attila represented a serious threat to the Eastern Empire but ultimately he was appeased and bought off with expensive annual tributes of gold by Theodosius II.

In the West successive emperors had retreated to Ravenna as barbarian control of Italy and its dominions had increased. Finally in 476 AD the last Western Roman Emperor Romulus Augustulus abdicated, effectively handing over power to the German born Odoacer. Many have viewed this event as marking the fall of the Western Empire. But the Eastern Empire endured and these events meant that Constantinople was unarguably the most significant and important city in the Empire.

Justinian

The reign of the Emperor Justinian I is widely regarded as one of the most important and successful phases of the Byzantine Empire. Justinian was born in Illyricum in 483 AD. His mother Vigilantia was the sister of the future Emperor Justin who, at this time, was an important general within the Empire. It was Justin who ensured that Justinian received an outstanding education. The young man became particularly well versed in Roman law and history and he had an intense personal interest in theological matters. His uncle Justin became Emperor in 518 AD and Justinian became consul three years later in 521 AD. Justinian enjoyed a successful career within the Empire and in 527 AD was made co-Emperor by his ailing uncle who died later that year.

Perhaps the single biggest influence on the life and reign of Justinian was his wife Theodora whom he married in 525 AD. In marrying her Justinian defied convention and generated a certain degree of scandal because she had formerly been an actress and worked as a prostitute. She had come from a low status background, her father being a bear-keeper in the Hippodrome of Constantinople. Her mother is thought to have also worked at the Hippodrome. The Hippodrome was the great circus of the city where games such as chariot racing were held and, in many ways, was the popular focus of city life. The circus had been a long-established aspect of Roman life and was a tradition that continued in the Eastern Empire. Over time the different competing teams or factions developed their own identities in ways that are perhaps comparable to modern day football teams. Within the world of chariot racing the two most important teams were the Greens and the Blues. Theodora's father had been employed by the Greens but, when he died, instead of his old job going to her mother's new husband, upon whom the family depended, it was granted to another man. In desperation her mother appealed to the sympathy of the rival Blues who then provided her stepfather with employment. This appears to have created a lifelong hatred of the Greens in Theodora who became an ardent supporter of the Blues. It also demonstrates the level of power that these rival circus factions exerted within the city. Justinian, before becoming Emperor, also supported the Blues and this may have been significant in their first meeting. At first it was inconceivable that Justinian could be Emperor whilst married to a woman of such low rank but his uncle, the Emperor Justin, conveniently passed a law that permitted retired actresses to marry into any level of society.

When Justinian became Emperor Theodora took an active and powerful role beside her husband who clearly valued her abilities and intelligence. He would often turn to her for advice and support throughout his reign. Rivals and enemies at the time wrote insultingly and viciously about Theodora but she proved a formidable and able Empress. Justinian himself also proved to be a shrewd judge of character and was greatly aided in his work as ruler by the capable and effective individuals he selected to help govern the Empire. Of particular note are John of Cappadocia who served as his finance minister and Tribonian, the Quaestor of the Sacred Palace, who was to help Justinian in a colossal review of Roman law.

John of Cappadocia was to help generate money for Justinian's war with Persia, his building programme and other government expenditure by introducing a far more effective and efficient tax system. He did much to spread taxes across all class boundaries, extracting money from both the wealthy and the poor and reducing the corruption that was rampant within the infrastructure of the Empire. However, his measures were extremely unpopular, perhaps precisely because they proved so successful, and, on a personal level, he was reviled for his, at times, cruel methods in implementing his new systems. Whilst he may not have been susceptible to fiscal corruption his personal conduct made him many enemies.

During Justinian's reign legislation was produced and enforced that suppressed and often persecuted non-Christian religions including the Manicheans and pre-Christian Hellenism. Justinian supported Nicaean Orthodoxy and acted zealously and continuously in its favour.

Roman Law

One of the greatest achievements of the reign of Justinian was his reformation and standardisation of Roman law. Before Justinian the Roman legal system had never been effectively organised and codified into a single coherent and universally understood form. By unifying the law, Justinian aimed to eliminate any contradictory or confusing aspects of the legal system and replaced it with a concise and effective series of statutes that would reflect the now prevailing Christian values of his reign.

His special legal advisor Tribonian was instrumental in this fundamental review of the law and its summation. It was completed in 529 AD and was ultimately to prove an important influence on modern European law.

The Hippodrome

The Hippodrome of Constantinople was one of the most important and popular buildings in the life of the imperial city. As we have seen, the chariot races that were held there had developed a greater significance and role within Byzantine culture than simply providing the populace with entertainment, although it certainly did serve that function. The first Hippodrome in the city had been built before its re-founding as Constantinople when it was still the provincial town of Byzantium. When Constantine had taken the decision to relocate the capital of the Empire his massive building plan had included a greatly enlarged

Hippodrome. Estimates put Constantine's redeveloped Hippodrome at 130 metres in width and 450 metres in length.

In 390 AD, during the reign of the Emperor Theodosius I, a colossal obelisk had been taken from the Temple of Karnak in the Egyptian city of Luxor and re-erected in the Hippodrome of Constantinople. Theodosius had it placed on the *spina* of the racetrack, a central barrier that it is tempting to think might correspond to the modern concept of the central reservation on a motorway! The obelisk had originally been set up in around 1490 BC by Tuthmosis III and provides another example of how the Emperors of Byzantium frequently appropriated artefacts from other cultures and eras to underline the glory and importance of their own empire. The obelisk was quarried from pink marble and the Emperor had it placed upon an elaborately carved base.

The base depicts Theodosius, surrounded by his subjects, presenting a wreath of victory from the imperial box. Astonishingly, the obelisk still stands today in the modern city of Istanbul, although the obelisk appears to have weathered rather better than the base that Theodosius had it set upon. There are of course striking parallels with the decision to transport this gigantic Egyptian pagan monument to a great capital at the heart of a Christian empire and the erection of Cleopatra's Needle on the Thames embankment in London during the Victorian era. Looking to the past for inspiration, it would seem, is nothing new. In fact, as we have seen, Constantine followed a similar policy and took an ancient artefact, called the Tripod of Plataea, from the prestigious Temple of Apollo at Delphi and ordered it to be set along the *spina* of the Hippodrome. The Tripod of Plataea was also known as the 'Serpent's Column' and had originally been created by the Greeks to thank Apollo for a famous victory over the Persians in 479 BC at Plataea.

As previously mentioned, the population of Constantinople supported differing teams who participated in the chariot races and other activities in the Hippodrome, the most powerful of whom became the Greens and Blues. The other teams had been the Whites and Reds but, over time, they lost influence and status until only the two dominant factions remained. The racetrack was also decorated with statues of well-known charioteers and their horses. Interestingly, a bronze sculpture of four horses that is today set upon the exterior of St Mark's Basilica in Venice originated in the Hippodrome of Constantinople, itself having become the victim of cultural plundering.

Nika Riots

The most serious civil disruptions in Constantinople during the reign of Justinian were the Nika riots that took place in 532 AD. These were the culmination of a series of events that had begun when members of the opposing circus factions, the Blues and the Greens, had been arrested after a riot broke out following the chariot races.

Several people were killed during the violence and members of the gangs were tried and convicted for their murders. Seven were sentenced to death. During the subsequent executions on 12 January, two gang members twice escaped death by hanging through a mixture of good fortune and error on the part of the hangmen. Supporters of the circus factions freed the men and helped them to escape and take shelter in the church of St Lawrence. The Prefect of the City had the church put under guard but just as quickly an angry mob, made up of supporters of the different teams, surrounded the church. One of the men inside the church was a Blue team supporter and the other a Green and the crowd united in shouting that they should both be freed.

When further games were held at the Hippodrome on 13 January, Justinian was met by an angry and volatile crowd as he declared the start of the games. The games at the Hippodrome were often used as a platform for the populace to express their feelings on matters of public interest but, on this occasion, Justinian found himself the focus of the combined anger of the usually divided circus factions. It was customary for the different teams to call out the name of their teams, 'Blue' or 'Green', followed by the Greek phrase 'Nika!' meaning 'win', 'victory' or 'conquer'. However, as the games went on, the cries of the crowd became a unified chant of 'Nika!' and were directed solely at the Emperor. The angry mob then spilled out onto the streets of Constantinople and headed for the City Prefect's palace where they overwhelmed the guards and set about freeing all the prisoners held inside it. They then set fire to the building and embarked on a trail of destruction through the city. Many important civic sites were burnt to the ground, including the churches of Hagia Sophia and St Irene.

The next day, the crowd demanded that John the Cappadocian and Tribonian be removed from their respective positions. Justinian, fearful of the consequences of refusing the demands, complied but these concessions failed to calm the situation.

Instead, the following day the mob demanded that a new Emperor be selected and chose a man named Probus who was a nephew of the former Emperor Anastasius.

Probus, perhaps fearing his selection as a potential rival to Justinian had already fled the city. Even when the Emperor offered an amnesty to the crowd on 18 January in the Hippodrome, the raging mob would not be calmed and they instead found another candidate called Hypatius. Like Probus, he was a nephew of the Emperor Anastastius and he was virtually forced by the crowd to become a replacement for Justinian. As a younger man the unfortunate Hypatius had served the Byzantine army as a general and he had no wish to supplant the Emperor.

When Justinian was on the point of leaving the city with his court, the Empress Theodora argued that he should stay and deal with the situation rather than taking the option of finding safety but losing the throne of Byzantium. The historian Procopius reports that the Empress rallied them by saying:

My opinion then is that the present time, above all others, is inopportune for flight, even though it bring safety... For one who has been an emperor it is unendurable to be a fugitive. May I never be separated from this purple, and may I not live that day on which those who meet me shall not address me as mistress. If, now it is your wish to save yourself, O Emperor, there is no difficulty. For we have money, and there is the sea, here the boats. However, consider whether it will not come about after you have been saved that you would not gladly exchange safety for death. For as myself, I approve a certain ancient saying that royalty is a good burial shroud.

(from Procopius, *History of the Wars*, I, xxiv, translated by HB Dewing, p219–230, slightly abridged and reprinted in Leon Barnard and Theodore B Hodges, *Readings in European History*, p.52–55).

Encouraged by the support of his formidable wife, Justinian commanded two of his generals, Belisarius and Mundus, to crush the insurrection. They trapped the mob of Blue and Green supporters in the Hippodrome, blocking its exits, and slaughtered those inside. It is said that as many as 30,000 were killed by Justinian's men. The unwilling surrogate Emperor Hypatius was summoned before Justinian who appears to have shown some sympathy to the older man's unhappy predicament. However, the Empress Theodora insisted that he be killed as a potential threat to the throne and Hypatius was executed. Those senators who had participated in or encouraged the rebellion were exiled or executed by Justinian.

Church of Hagia Sophia

The reconstruction of the church of Hagia Sophia, burnt to the ground during the Nika riots, became an immediate priority of the Emperor Justinian. Taking its name from the Greek word 'Sophia' meaning 'Holy Wisdom' or the 'Holy Wisdom of God', the church had originally been planned by Constantine the Great. However, it was his son Constantius who actually built the first incarnation of the church in about 360 AD. This building had been destroyed in 404 AD during earlier riots that focused on the expulsion of the controversial figure of John Chrysostom. Theodosius II had then rebuilt the church during his reign.

When Justinian undertook to rebuild Hagia Sophia in 532 AD he planned not simply a reconstruction of the original design of the church but an incredible re-imagining that would make it a wonder of the ancient world. Justinian devised its construction with two architects named Isidore of Miletus and Anthemius of Tralles. Both men are thought to have studied in Egypt during their careers and Anthemius had constructed other churches for Justinian that had greatly impressed the Emperor. It is thought that Justinian began planning a reconstruction of Hagia Sophia before its destruction during the riots because it became such an elaborate and sumptuous design that the few weeks it took to begin rebuilding would not have been enough for such a vast plan to take shape. In scale it was the largest Christian structure anyone had attempted to build and it was richly decorated with marble from various parts of the Empire.

Incredible effort was also expended on covering much of the interior in rich mosaics and on elaborate and costly church fittings. But perhaps its most impressive feature and the aspect of the building's architectural design that would have the greatest influence on future generations was its huge dome. The central dome of Hagia Sophia is 56 metres high and 31 metres in diameter. Its builders managed to create the illusion that the dome floats almost without weight upon a series of 40 windows that allow in light, further illuminating the brightly coloured interior. The weight of the dome is carried on four great pendentives, triangular structures that rest on the rectangular base of the church and it is further distributed by interior ribs within the dome that extend downwards to the floor of the building. The dome design is continued in the eastern and western sections of the building in an incredible marriage of aesthetic beauty and structural control.

The church of Hagia Sopia, constructed by Justinian, is often considered to be a defining masterpiece in Byzantine architecture and it established an artistic style of its own that has subsequently influenced Islamic, Eastern Orthodox and Roman Catholic building styles. Justinian is famously reported to have said, 'Solomon, I have surpassed you', at the ceremony of dedication of the church of St Sophia in December 537 AD.

Reconquest of North Africa and Italy

In the wake of the successful suppression of the Nika riots, Justinian appointed Belisarius to the task of reconquering territories of the Western Empire that had been lost. A peace treaty had been agreed between the Byzantine Empire and the Persians in 532 AD which meant that Justinian was now able to turn his military attention and ambitions to the countries in the west of the Mediterranean. It was Justinian's aim to restore those territories lost to the Empire and have them ruled by a single Byzantine Emperor from Constantinople. Belisarius proved to be a brilliant general and successfully recaptured North Africa from the Vandals in 533 AD. Justinian accorded Belisarius a triumphant parade at the Hippodrome of Constantinople where war booty in the form of riches and human captives were shown off to the population of the city. Many of those Vandals taken to Constantinople were pressed into military service in the legions. Belisarius and Justinian then undertook the reconquest of Sicily and Italy, capturing the city of Rome in 536 AD. However, it was to be a further four years before Belisarius succeeded in capturing the Gothic capital of Ravenna in the north of Italy in 540 AD. In the event the celebrations following the success of Belisarius were to prove extremely short-lived due to renewed fighting in the East and the general's subsequent recall by Justinian to defend the Empire against the Persians.

Bubonic Plague

Between 541 AD and 542 AD the Byzantine Empire was hit by a widespread and massively destructive outbreak of bubonic plague. It is thought that the plague may have begun in Egypt or Ethiopia and been carried to Constantinople on ships supplying the capital with grain. Constantinople was heavily dependent on these shipments of grain that came largely from Egypt and huge granaries had been built to store it that in turn became a home to the rats that carried the plague.

The historian Procopius recorded that as many as 10,000 people a day were killed by the plague at its height and the population of the city was unable to keep up with the normal burial of the dead. The enormous toll of the disease led to a lack of people to maintain the production and distribution of food and this, in turn, led to a secondary crisis in the city. The Emperor Justinian also fell ill with the plague and the Empress Theodora ruled temporarily in his stead. The plague weakened the Byzantine Empire at the point when Justinian had just reconquered territories in the West that had previously been lost and it made retaining them impossible. In 548 AD the Empress Theodora died and the later years of Justinian's reign were at times difficult and testing. However, the Emperor continued to rule until his death in 565 AD and was succeeded by his nephew Justin.

The Rise of Islam

The reign of Justin II saw the Avars invade Thrace and successfully resist the army the Emperor sent against them. Justin was forced to pay a tribute to them to ensure peace. A Germanic people called the Lombards invaded much of Italy. However, Ravenna, Naples, Calabria, Sicily and parts of the Venetian lagoon remained in Imperial hands. When Justin died in 578 AD, he was succeeded by Tiberius who had failed to defeat the Avar forces. His reign was brief, ending with his death in 582 AD, but, before he died, he appointed a general called Maurice as his successor. Perhaps the major achievements of Maurice's reign were the creation of the Exarchates of Carthage and Ravenna in an attempt to retain Byzantine territories. Both were ruled by an Exarch, or provincial governor, who had ultimate power over all matters within the imperial domains. Continuing conflict with the Avars and dissatisfaction with his reign led the army to revolt against him in 602 AD. A centurion called Phokas was elected from the ranks to replace him. Made Emperor with the help of the Greens, Phokas ordered the execution of Maurice and his family.

Heraclius

The rebel centurion Phokas faced opposition to his reign as Emperor in 608 AD when Heraclius the Elder challenged his right to the throne. Heraclius had been an important general serving under the Emperor Maurice against the Persian Empire and had subsequently been given the position of Exarch of Africa. His son Heraclius, who had grown up in Africa, sailed with an army to Constantinople in 609 AD, stopping along the way to gain support for his challenge to the throne. Niketas, cousin of Heraclius, seized control of Egypt in the same year. Many important figures within Constantinople, including Priscus, the son-in-law of Phokas, switched loyalties to Heraclius and he was able to take the city with little difficulty. He was declared Emperor and executed Phokas himself. Heraclius was officially crowned on 5 October 610 AD at the Chapel of St Stephen within the imperial palace and he also married his betrothed Fabia on the same day. His wife took the new name of Eudocia on becoming Empress.

Although the ascent of Heraclius to the position of Emperor had been assured and successful, he found himself in control of an Empire in crisis. The Balkans had been invaded by the Avars and, in the East, Chosroes II, a former ally of the Emperor Maurice, had declared war on the Empire. The Persians successfully captured Damascus in 613 AD, Jerusalem in 614 AD and all of Egypt in 616 AD. The capture of Jerusalem proved particularly shocking to the Byzantines because the Persians brutally suppressed a violent Christian uprising in the city and burnt the Church of the Holy Sepulchre to the ground. They also seized the fragment of the True Cross and many other important relics and carried them back to their capital of Ctesiphon. The Christians had killed many Jews and Persians in the initial uprising and, in reprisal, Jews and Persians united in killing many thousands of Christians. Whilst the loss of the city and many of its relics and shrines horrified the rulers and citizens of Constantinople the capture of Egypt, one of the primary suppliers of grain to the city, was to prove disastrous.

The Persians made major inroads into Anatolia, modern day Turkey and even reached the town of Chalcedon that lay across the Bosphorous from Constantinople itself. Famously and eerily, it is said that the inhabitants of Constantinople were able to see the fires of the Persian soldiers reflected in the sea on the horizon at night. With the Avars dominating Greece, the major food sources for Constantinople had been cut off. The situation became so dire that, in 618 AD, Heraclius seriously considered abandoning Constantinople and retreating to his African home of Carthage in order to regroup his forces and renew his attack on his enemies. Many have argued that this was, in fact, a sensible and viable alternative to the situation that he was confronted with but the Patriarch of the city, Sergius, begged and implored the Emperor to stay. In the end Heraclius agreed to remain and immediately set about rebuilding and reorganising the lands still left to the Empire.

Drawing on his own experiences and life in Roman Carthage, Heraclius divided the remaining Byzantine territories into four great areas or 'Themes'. This term is derived from the Greek word *thema* that describes a division of troops. The *thema* was placed under the command of a military governor known as a *strategos*. Heraclius also developed the idea of giving gifts of land to men in return for hereditary military service. Previously, Emperors had recruited armies for specific campaigns and they were often composed of mercenaries or barbarian troops with divided or loose loyalties. Now the territories would be defended by armed forces with a vested interest in fighting for their homes, land and families. As mentioned above such a system had been in place in the Exarchate of Carthage and it had also been used within the Exarchate of Ravenna. Once again it proved to be an effective strategy.

After implementing these new measures, Heraclius personally led a war fleet south against the Persians in 621 AD. He was the first Emperor to lead an army against an enemy since Theodosius I. Travelling southwards along the coast of Asia Minor, the fleet landed at the Bay of Issus and the army then marched north and inland to meet the Persians in battle. The Byzantines proved victorious and the next few years were spent campaigning against the Persians. However, in 626 AD, the Avars laid siege to Constantinople itself. They were beaten back and Persian attempts to attack across the Bosphorous were also successfully repulsed by the Byzantine navy. Heraclius then forged allegiances with the Khazars of the Caucasus and other neighbouring peoples and set up headquarters at Trebizond. His alliances meant that he was able to lead his army deep into enemy territory in what is now modern day Iraq. In 627 AD Heraclius won a significant victory against the Persian forces. Their king Chosroes II initially refused to cease hostilities but he was himself overthrown by his own son who finally made peace with Heraclius. Those territories that had belonged to the Byzantine Empire were restored to them as were the relics taken from Jerusalem, including the True Cross. This was seen very much as a Christian victory over pagan forces and Heraclius began to term himself as a Basileus, a Greek term for king, dropping the Roman or Latin term Augustus. In many ways Heraclius set a precedent for giving the Eastern Empire an increasingly Greek character since all subsequent emperors adopted this title. He also made Greek the official language of the Empire, moving away from the use of Latin. In 631 AD Heraclius personally oversaw the return of the True Cross to the Church of the Holy Sepulchre in Jerusalem.

Having achieved so much to stabilize the Empire in the face of external dangers, Heraclius now attempted to heal the internal religious rifts that were still causing division. The provinces that had been conquered by the Persians had been shown religious toleration by their occupiers and the Monophysite Christians, who had rejected the findings of the council of Chalcedon of 451 AD, had grown in numbers and strength. They believed that Christ had one nature, which was divine. The Patriarch of Constantinople, Sergius, attempted to create a new theological formula that could be accepted by both the Orthodox Church and the Monophysites. His new religious doctrine was known as Monothelitism and argued that Christ was both perfect man and perfect God but possessed only one single energy. The formula met with initial success and was received favourably by most of the patriarchs. It was even accepted by Pope Honorius in Rome. However, its most vociferous opponent was the Patriarch of Jerusalem, Sophronius, who proclaimed loudly in 634 AD that it was heresy and rejected it outright. Sophronius persuaded many to his point of view and the popularity of the compromise formula faded away.

These arguments over the exact nature of Christ, that had so absorbed the different factions of the Church, were soon to be usurped in importance by the arrival of a new and unexpected threat to the stability of the Empire in the form of the armies of Islam. Arabic Muslim forces invaded Syria and conquered Damascus in the same year that Sophronius proclaimed Monothelitism to be heresy and the Byzantine force raised by Heraclius was defeated. The Emperor now despaired of the situation and had the True Cross that he had only recently returned to Jerusalem transported to Constantinople where he also took refuge. By 637 AD Jerusalem was under siege by the Muslims and surrendered the following year. Patriarch Sophronius, who had so vocally challenged the doctrine of Monothelitism, was forced to hand the city over to the Caliph Omar.

Heraclius' later years were afflicted by failing physical and mental health and his second marriage to his niece

Martina caused much turmoil and scandal. Some of their children were born with disabilities or died when they were very young. For many this was a punishment from God and it seems likely that Heraclius himself began to feel that this was true. His victory over the Persians had left both empires weakened and unable to meet the new threat of Islam and his attempts to bring peace to the Church had failed. However, Heraclius persisted with the doctrine of Monothelitism and the Patriarch of Constantinople Sergius offered a revised version of the theological formula. Now it was said that Christ was in possession of two natures, perfect man and perfect God, but had a single will. This formula was put forward as an imperial decree known as the Ekthesis and initially met with widespread support.

However, this time it was the turn of the western Pope John IV to rebel and he rejected the formula. When Heraclius died in 641 AD it seemed that many of his achievements had been in vain. But it was to be his re-organisation of the military, particularly in Asia Minor, that would stop the spread of the Arab invasion and ensured the survival of the Byzantine Empire for centuries to come.

Mohammed and the Rise of Islam

Before proceeding further with the story of Byzantium, it is important and necessary to examine the beginnings and development of Islam, a faith system that would ultimately determine the fate of the Byzantine Empire and emerge as a major world religion. The religion of Islam was to provide the previously divided Arabic tribes with a single unity of purpose that they had not previously possessed and galvanise their people into a power with which to be reckoned. The founder of Islam was the prophet Mohammed whom Muslims consider to be the most important and final prophet of God. Mohammed was born around 570 AD in the town of Mecca in Northern Arabia. He became an orphan as a young boy and was raised firstly by his grandfather and then by his uncle. In Mohammed's youth the town of Mecca was an important site of pilgrimage focused on a stone temple filled with idols. The temple is today known as the Kaaba and it is the holiest site in the Muslim world. Under the influence of his uncle, Mohammed became a merchant and travelled to Syria. He married a widow who was older than him and started a family. It is believed by Muslims that, in 610 AD, Mohammed was visited by the Angel Gabriel in a cave near Mecca where he customarily spent time in contemplation. He was instructed by Gabriel to recite a series of verses that were given by God. Mohammed received these verses for the rest of his life and they were posthumously collected together and written down as the Quran, a term that translates as 'recitation'. Following on from his revelations from the Angel Gabriel, Mohammed began preaching and emphasised the importance of belief in a single God. His monotheistic stance set him at odds with many in Mecca and Mohammed and those who followed him were persecuted.

Around 622 AD Mohammed revealed that he had been

taken on a night journey by the Angel Gabriel, known as the Isra and the Miraj. During the Isra Gabriel had taken him to Jerusalem. It was here that he ascended to heaven from the site of the Dome of the Rock in the second part of the journey, the Miraj. Mohammed reported that he had spoken to other prophets including Moses and Jesus. Mohammed finally left Mecca with his followers to settle in the city of Medina in a journey termed the Hijra or 'migration'. Armed forces from Mecca repeatedly attacked the Muslims at Medina but were driven away. Mohammed finally led his followers against the city of Mecca and conquered it. The idols were taken from the Kaaba and the people of Mecca converted to Islam. Many other Arabic tribes followed suit and, after Mohammed died in 632 AD, Islam continued to grow, becoming an empire in its own right led by the caliphs who succeeded the Prophet.

Greek Fire

An excellent example of how the Byzantines were able to innovate in order to overcome crises is their development and use of a devastatingly effective chemical weapon known as 'Greek fire'. Its importance was such that its formula was a state secret guarded by the Emperor and it is now lost to us. Contemporary accounts describe a flammable, sticky incendiary liquid that burned with incredible intensity and that water could not extinguish. In fact, contact with water often served only to spread the liquid and it would continue burning even when it became submerged. It was used most successfully, although not exclusively, by the Byzantine navy which, with often terrifying results, propelled the liquid, under pressure, through metal siphons and towards enemy ships. Its sticky nature meant that it would cling to the hulls of wooden boats, their sails and oars and, most horrifically, to their crews. Enemies of the Byzantines came to fear and dread the terrible fire inflicted on them and even the mere threat of its use, when Byzantine ships equipped with the ingenious siphon devices were sighted, could be enough to cause opponents to flee in terror.

Its qualities have been compared to that of the vicious modern chemical weapon napalm, an agent whose use caused so much horror and revulsion during the Vietnam War. However, it may surprise some to know that the use of chemically based incendiary weapons in the ancient world, particularly in the East, was fairly well known. The abundance of oil and its flammable qualities had led to much experimentation in the production of substances with military applications.

The contemporary chronicler Theophanes ascribes the invention of Greek fire in 670 AD to a Syrian refugee by the name of Kallinikos who had fled the Muslim invasion of his country and sought sanctuary in Constantinople. The primary reason for the effectiveness of Greek fire was the development of the system of propulsion that seems to have resembled that of a soda siphon and allowed the Byzantines to use the mixture in a way that would resemble the use of a modern weapon such as a flamethrower. It may be that the liquid ignited through pressure as it was expelled through the siphon. It is thought that its primary component was naptha, 'originally used as an incendiary poured over or hurled at besiegers in Mesopotamia, and later in firebombs catapulted by mangonels invented in Damascus and used by Muslims to bombard fortifications'. (Adrienne Mayor, *Greek Fire, Poison Arrows, and Scorpion Bombs*, p.241) The earliest recorded usage of Greek fire by the Byzantines can actually be dated to 513 AD but it was the invention of a system of brass tubes and cauldrons that could produce controlled projections of the fluid that transformed it into a far more formidable armament.

The importance of Greek fire as an effective weapon is reflected in the fact that the Byzantine navy came to possess a specific group of sailors who were responsible for its use called the *siphonarioi*. Their role in the Byzantine navy was, in effect, not dissimilar to that of a gunner on a modern naval ship. Greek fire was used with great success during the seven-year-long Arab siege of Constantinople from 670 AD to 677 AD, destroying and driving away the blockading enemy ships. It was also to prove crucial in saving Constantinople in 718 AD from another attack by the Arab fleet. Many have argued that the Byzantine Empire owed its survival, particularly in its later period, to this fearsome weapon. An interesting testimony to the use of Greek fire during the crusades was recorded in the memoirs of Jean de Joinville. So terrifying and formidable was Greek fire to the men with whom he was fighting to hold a stronghold that, every time it was hurled at them, they dropped to their knees in prayer. He describes events in the thirteenth century during a siege:

> This was the fashion of the Greek fire: it came on as broad in front as a vinegar cask, and the tail of fire that trailed behind it was as big as a great spear: and it made such a noise as it came, that it sounded like the thunder of heaven. It looked like a dragon flying through the air. Such a bright light did it cast, that one could see all over the camp as though it were day, by reason of the great mass of fire, and the brilliance of the light that it shed.
>
> (Ethel Wedgwood [ed.]),
> *The Memoirs of the Lord of Joinville*, p. 39).

Constans II

Following the death of the Emperor Heraclius, the Empire was thrown into a period of confusion and infighting that seems largely to have been the work of his second wife Martina. Finally, she was banished by the senate to the island of Rhodes and the grandson of Heraclius, Constans II, was proclaimed Emperor in 642 AD at the age of just eleven. The senate ruled in his stead until he reached adulthood. His reign began with the loss of most of Egypt that Martina had surrendered to the Arabian armies. This represented a serious loss to the Byzantines and the Arab forces pushed on through North Africa where they won a battle against Gregory the Exarch of Carthage.

Under the reign of Othman, who had succeeded Omar as Caliph after the latter's death, the Arabian forces began the process of building a naval fleet. As a people used to life in the desert this was a new and ambitious undertaking and one in which they were to prove very successful. In 649 AD they attacked the Byzantine island of Cyprus and caused considerable damage to the capital and its port although they did not capture the whole island. Cyprus was an important naval base for the Byzantine Empire and this strike was designed to cause as much damage and disruption as possible. The Arabian navy went on to attack Rhodes in 654 AD, which they captured along with the nearby island of Kos. Constans II led a fleet against the Arabs in 655 AD but was defeated.

However, events turned in favour of the Byzantines when the Islamic world was thrown into uproar by the assassination in 656 AD of the Caliph Othman. A period of internal feuding ensued between the Muslim governor of Syria, Muawiya, and Ali, grandson of the Prophet himself. Constans took the opportunity to strengthen the defences of the Empire during the cessation of hostilities, particularly those in Anatolia, but, by 661 AD, Muawiya had gained control. Arab attacks on the Empire were renewed and, by 662 AD, Constans II had taken the dramatic step of apparently abandoning Constantinople for the safety of the West. Constans based himself in Sicily whilst his wife and sons remained in Constantinople. The Muslim naval forces under Muawiya gained an increasing control over the Anatolian coastal waters and finally besieged Constantinople in 670

AD. The defence of the city was left to Constantine IV, son of Constans II. The use and effectiveness of Greek fire, as we have seen, proved to be pivotal in the eventual defeat of the Arab navy and it finally abandoned the siege in 678 AD.

In the aftermath of this victory Constantine IV attempted to resolve the disputes that were continuing to cause division in the Church. His father Constans II had continued to espouse the doctrinal position of Monothelitism, first put forward in the reign of the Emperor Heraclius, and this had caused further friction between Rome and Constantinople when Pope Theodore had opposed it. Rome had originally supported the Christological formula but, when Constans II produced a decree called the Typos in 648 AD, the papacy rejected it. Central to the opposition had been a monk called Maximos the Confessor who agitated against the Monothelite line and gained the support of Pope Martin who came to power in 649 AD. Constans saw the opposition as a direct challenge to his power and had both Maximos and Martin sent into exile, quashing the dissent but creating a growing sense of enmity. Constantine IV aimed to overcome these problems at a General Council of the Church in 680 AD. The Monothelite policy was condemned and it appeared that the Eastern and Western Churches were reconciled.

The Fall of Carthage

When Constantine IV died in 685 AD his son Justinian II succeeded him. Constantine had negotiated a payment of tribute to the Byzantine Empire with the Caliph Muawiya and this was continued when Muawiya was succeeded as Caliph by Abdul Malik. The tribute was said to be as much as 1,000 nomismata a day – the equivalent of 5,000 pounds of gold per year. In addition, payments of horses and slaves were made. Justinian II and Caliph Abdul Malik also agreed to share revenues generated by Cyprus, Armenia and Iberia. Justinian II also agreed to evacuate the tribe known as the Mardaites from Syria where they had fought successfully against the Arab armies on more than one occasion. They were to be moved to Anatolia. In 688 AD Justinian continued this policy of repopulating Anatolia in order to strengthen the Empire's borders. The city of Thessaloniki had become dominated by tribes of Slavs and Justinian led an army against them that re-established imperial rule there. In the wake of this mission the emperor arranged for the transportation of many Slavs to Anatolia where they were resettled. However, in 691 AD, large numbers of Slavs joined the Arabian forces and the following year the Byzantines lost Armenia after suffering a defeat at Sebastopolis. Justinian had made himself unpopular with both peasants and aristocrats through his high taxes and his often cruel methods in extracting them. A revolt in 695 AD saw a soldier from the aristocratic classes called Leontius proclaimed as Emperor, supported by the powerful faction of the Blues. Justinian was sent into exile but not before his nose had been mutilated to prevent him from becoming Emperor again. (It was a requirement of Byzantine society that an Emperor should be without physical defects in order to rule.)

Leontius was to fare little better than Justinian and, when Carthage fell to the Saracens in 698 AD, he himself was usurped by a rebel called Tiberius, supported by the Greens. His nose was also cut and he was forced into monastic exile. Whilst he was in exile, Justinian had managed to persuade the Bulgar King Tervel to support his reinstatement and they marched on Constantinople at the head of a Bulgar and Slav force. Tiberius fled the city but was later recaptured and executed. During the later part of his reign Justinian took to covering his mutilated face with a nose made of gold, an act that might have earned him the Bond-like epithet of the Emperor with the Golden Nose. In 711 AD he was once again overthrown and this time executed by an Armenian general called Philippicus. Between 711 AD and 717 AD Byzantine leadership under-went a period of turmoil that was finally ended by the acclamation of Leo III as Emperor.

Iconoclasm

Leo III had been a governor of the Theme of Anatolikon and was Syrian in origin. Something of a schemer, he had made deals with the Arabs that they should retreat from imperial land and so earn him his acclamation as Emperor. The pay-off was to be the eventual surrender of Constantinople but, in the event, Leo had simply bought himself time to secure the city. The Arabian forces besieged the city from 717 AD to 718 AD but were beaten back.

However, despite this military success, the reign of Leo

III is now most associated with the doctrine of iconoclasm. The word 'iconoclasm' means literally 'the smashing or breaking of icons' and it was given to a religious movement that saw the worship of icons as being idolatrous. Why this controversy should have appeared during this period has been the source of considerable debate.

Many have ascribed iconoclasm to the growing cultural influence of Islam and to the belief that the worship of images equates to the worship of false idols, forbidden by the Second Commandment in the Law of Moses. Where images of Christ, the Virgin and the Saints had become widespread and revered in Byzantine culture, Islam rejected pictures and more commonly made use of decorative calligraphy and written sources in its holy places. The Bishop of Nakoleia and others from Anatolia had begun agitating against the use of icons but they were resisted by the patriarch of Constantinople, Germanos I. In 726 AD Leo ordered that an important icon of Christ, known as the Chalke, which was set above the doorway to the imperial palace should be removed. This action caused widespread unrest but the Emperor was not to be dissuaded. On 7 January 730 AD, Leo III issued a decree ordering the destruction of icons. In the West the decree was met with consternation and anger and Pope Gregory II condemned iconoclasm. A Western synod in 731 AD decreed that any attempt to remove holy objects would be punished by excommunication, a clear threat to Leo. Once again the Church was split by internal division and the tensions between East and West would continue into the future.

The Great Schism

The policy of iconoclasm imposed by the Emperor Leo III was to continue during the reign of his son, Constantine V. He inherited the throne after his father's death in 741 AD but was almost immediately challenged for his title, in 742, by Artabasdus, his brother-in-law. Artabasdus succeeded in his challenge to Constantine V and restored the worship of icons. However, only a year later, Constantine V was back on the throne and once again the use of icons was banned. During the reign of Constantine V hostilities between the Empire and the Bulgars increased. Although the Emperor achieved a number of victories against them, the Bulgars would remain a threat to the Empire and shape its development for several centuries.

Despite his success against the Bulgars, Constantine V neglected the defence of the Byzantine Exarchate of Ravenna and it finally fell to the Lombards in 751 AD. Pope Stephen II forged allegiances with the Franks who, under the leadership of Pepin the Short, recaptured lands that had been lost to the Lombards and put them under papal authority in 756 AD. Constantine V was succeeded by his son Leo IV, an iconoclast like his father. Upon his early death from tuberculosis, his wife Irene ruled in his stead since their son Constantine VI was still a child. Irene was the only woman to rule the Empire as a regent in her own right and her time in power was characterised by a return to the veneration of icons and by her domination of her son Constantine VI. He deposed her briefly but Irene returned to power and Constantine was blinded for his insubordination, dying of his injuries in 797 AD.

In the West, Charles, the son of Pepin the Short, was crowned 'Emperor of the Romans' by Pope Leo III in 800 AD. The decision to name Charles Emperor caused consternation among the people of Constantinople who considered their own Emperors to be the direct successors to the Roman Empire. Charles, better known to history as Charlemagne, made an offer of marriage to Irene but she was deposed before she had time to accept.

She was replaced by the Logothete of the Treasury, Nicephorus I. As Regent, Nicephorus improved the finances of the Empire but he was killed in battle against the Bulgars in 811 AD. His son Stauracius was injured at the same time and, unable to rule, died shortly afterwards without an heir. The throne then passed to the husband of the daughter of Nicephorus, Michael Rhangabe. After numerous failures in battle, he abdicated in favour of Leo V. Ruling from 813 AD to 820 AD, Leo re-instituted iconoclasm, largely as a measure to pacify soldiers from the East in Constantinople who had been driven from their homes by the Saracens and were iconoclasts.

He was violently overthrown by a close friend, Michael II, who, during the course of his reign, overcame a virtual civil war instigated by Thomas the Slav but also lost the island of Crete to Arab pirates. When Michael II died in 829 AD he left his son Theophilus to rule as Basileus. The reign of Theophilus was characterised by ongoing conflicts with Muslim forces and his death in 842 AD effectively marked the end of iconoclasm. During the following reign of his wife Theodora and his son Michael III, the public veneration of icons resumed. In private, it had probably never really ended.

In 865 AD, Michael III succeeded in forcing the Bulgar Khan Boris and his people to adopt Orthodox Christianity. The Khan was baptised in 865 AD in Constantinople. During this period theological controversy raged between the churches of Rome and Constantinople over what was termed the *Filioque* dispute. In the Eastern Church the Holy Ghost was said to proceed from the Father but, in the West, an insertion had been added to the Nicene Creed. The addition was the word *Filioque* meaning 'and the Son' and had now become accepted in the Western Church. For the Eastern Church, this was heresy and a challenge to its authority. Once again Rome and Constantinople were vying with one another for religious supremacy.

Macedonian Emperors

Although Michael III gained a reputation as a brave and accomplished soldier and as a military leader, he was a figure who has come to be associated with personal dissipation. He spent much of his reign in the pursuit of pleasure and is sometimes referred to as 'Michael the Sot' for his wild and drunken behaviour. At times the Emperor appeared more interested in chariot racing than in ruling and, to a certain extent, it could be argued he delegated responsibilities in order to focus on the hedonistic carousing that he so enjoyed. In 866 AD, Michael III took the fateful step of raising a personal friend, known as Basil the Macedonian, to the level of co-Emperor. Basil's sobriquet is misleading because he was, in fact, Armenian in origin. He was one of many Armenians whose family had been settled by the Empire within Thrace, close to the capital. However, in later raids by the Bulgars, many resettled Armenian families, together with many Macedonians, had been carried off to a region north of the river Danube and they came to be collectively referred to as 'Macedonian'. Basil was from a humble background and, in all likelihood, met Michael III through one of the Emperor's pursuits, such as chariot racing. Having gained Michael's friendship, he advanced rapidly. For a short time, Basil was happy to indulge the Emperor's whims. In the end, Michael's extreme debauchery led his former friend to plot against him. As on so many other occasions in Byzantine history, the reign of the Emperor was to end in his bloody assassination. In 867 AD, Basil, with a group of supporters, murdered Michael whilst he was lying in the palace in a drunken stupor. In doing so, Basil established the so-called Macedonian dynasty that was to continue the imperial line until 1025 AD and included the reigns of Leo VI, Alexander, Constantine VII Porphyrogenitus, Romanus I

Lecapenus, Romanus II, Nicephorus II Phokas and John I Tzimisces.

Basil the Bulgar Slayer

In many ways the Emperor Basil II, known to posterity as the Bulgar Slayer, was to prove to be one of the most successful and remarkable regents in the later history of the Byzantine Empire. He was born in 958 AD the son of the Emperor Romanus II who made him a co-regent while he was still an infant. Unfortunately, Romanus died when Basil was only five years old and his mother remarried a general, known as Nicephorus II Phokas, who ruled in his stead from 963 AD until his death in 969 AD. Following Nicephorus' death he was succeeded by the Emperor John I Tzimisces who ruled until 976 AD. In that same year, Basil II became senior Emperor at the age of 18.

However, for the first nine years of his reign, Basil was dominated by his great-uncle, the eunuch Basil Lecapenus, who had been president of the senate for many years and, apparently unwilling to give up control of the Empire, continued to wield considerable power. Basil II also faced challenges from other rivals to the throne who contested the later tradition of familial succession to the throne in favour of the acclamation of Emperors by the army or the seizing of power. As early as 976 AD Bardus Sclerus, an important figure in the army, was declared as Basileus or Emperor by his own men and besieged the capital. The eunuch Basil Lecapenus took the decision to entrust the defence of the city to Bardas Phocas, himself a potential rival to the throne, who none the less succeeded in suppressing Sclerus' rebellion.

In the meantime Basil II appears to have played something of a waiting game, familiarising himself with the machinations of the Empire and developing his skills as an administrator and soldier. Finally, in 985 AD, the overbearing behaviour of his uncle proved too much and Basil II had him arrested, his property seized and sent him into exile.

It was not long before Basil II faced his first major crisis as ruler when Tsar Samuel of Bulgaria invaded the Byzantine province of Thessaly and captured Larissa, its main city. The capture of the city and the subsequent treatment of its citizens was said to have been particularly cruel and brutal and Basil II was determined to punish the Tsar and his forces. It was to be the first major campaign in which Basil led the army personally but, unfortunately, it was also to be his most disastrous. He made the tactical error of leading the army through a mountain pass known as Trajan's Gate to the city of Sardica but calling a halt in order to let his rearguard catch up. This gave the Tsar an opportunity to deploy troops into the mountains. The siege of Sardica was unsuccessful and Basil led his army back through the pass of Trajan's Gate and straight into an ambush.

The army was routed although Basil and a small remainder of the troops survived. The humiliation of his defeat was to create a terrible hatred in Basil of the Bulgarian Empire and a desire for future revenge. His defeat also convinced Bardas Phocas that the time was right to challenge Basil as Emperor. He marched on Constantinople and set up camp at Chrysopolis on the Asian shore of the Bosphorous in 989 AD.

In response, Basil called upon the aid of Prince Vladimir I of Kiev. Vladimir agreed to send a force of 6,000 to help Basil but added a condition that Basil should give his own sister Anna in marriage to him. Basil agreed but insisted that the heathen prince convert to Orthodox Christianity. The rebel Bardas Phocas was defeated with the assistance of the Varangian troops sent by Vladimir who were of Viking descent. Prince Vladimir kept his word and embraced the Orthodox faith and set about converting his people to the new faith, thus enlarging the Eastern Church and shaping the future of Russia and Eastern Europe.

Following the fall of a number of Byzantine towns to Bulgar forces, Basil turned his attentions to their recapture and the strengthening of defences, notably in Thessalonica. However, in 995 AD, Basil was forced to lead an army to Syria against the Muslim Arabs. He was able to rescue the city of Aleppo and secured most of Syria under Byzantine control. Basil also took great steps to undermine the power and land holdings of the great Anatolian barons of whom Phokas and Sclerus had been two. These vast estates were broken up and restored to the poor families from which they had been taken unlawfully. The importance of these peasant farmers was that they were the source of the majority of the manpower for the army and the restitution of their rights diminished the power of the barons and strengthened Basil's position.

Basil focused on campaigning against the Bulgars from 1000 AD onwards with the most significant battle in this ongoing struggle taking place in 1014 AD. At the Battle of Clidion Basil managed to defeat the Bulgarian army and, although Tsar Samuel escaped, as many as 15,000 other prisoners were captured. Basil punished the captives terribly, blinding every 99 men out of 100. Those who were left unmutilated were forced to lead their blinded comrades back to their Tsar who is said to have collapsed on their arrival. He died shortly afterwards, apparently from the shock caused by this experience. Although the Bulgarians were to fight on, they were finally defeated in 1018 AD and Basil's wars against the Bulgars earned him the nickname of *Boulgaroctonos* meaning 'Bulgar-slayer'. Basil also negotiated the passing of Armenia back to Byzantine control and Byzantine forces managed to recapture territories in the south of Italy. He was planning to retake Sicily when he died on 15 December 1025 AD. Although his achievements were many and he left the Empire in a considerably stronger state than he had inherited it, Basil never married and left no heir to the throne. For this reason, it is often argued that Basil's rule, successful in so many ways, did not halt the subsequent overall decline of the Byzantine Empire.

The Great Schism

The fate of the island of Sicily was to generate conflicts over and above its importance as a former territory that the

Byzantines hoped to reconquer. Just as the island of Malta proved to be a point of key importance to the British during the Second World War, Sicily was considered by the Byzantines to be of strategic significance as a base to exert control in the Mediterranean.

However, Muslim Arabs contested the Byzantines for control of the island with a number of raids against the island that became a full-scale invasion in 827 AD. By 831 AD the city of Palermo had fallen to the Arabs but Byzantine forces on the island hung on grimly until as late as 878 AD when the capital of Syracuse was lost. Following the death of Basil II an attempt was made to recapture the island but proved unsuccessful and foundered in 1041 AD.

In the following years Sicily drew the attention of Normans with an eye to establishing new kingdoms. Some Norman warriors had taken military service in the south of Italy under the Lombards and Byzantine authorities. The Byzantines still held an important base in southern Italy at Bari. However, it was not long before groups of Normans began to seek power for themselves. One such group, led by Robert Guiscard, took to raiding in the area and attacked the city of Benevento, controlled at that time by the papacy. In 1053 AD Pope Leo IX led an army against the Normans but was defeated and taken captive at the Battle of Civitate. The failure of Byzantine forces to support the army of the Pope led to much resentment amongst his supporters. Ironically, the Byzantine Emperor Constantine IX Monomachus and Argyrus, commander of the Byzantine forces in southern Italy, were in agreement that the papacy and the Empire should join forces against the Normans.

However, they were opposed in this policy by the Patriarch of Constantinople, Michael Cerularius, who believed that support for the papacy would only result in the loss of the power and prestige of the Eastern Church in the region. He became involved in a stinging dispute with the Pope, criticising him for allowing the Normans to introduce Latin customs in Greek churches. Whilst the Emperor Constantine IX Monomachus continued to work towards an alliance of the Byzantine and Latin worlds, Pope Leo IX dispatched papal representatives to Constantinople with a letter addressed to the Emperor in which he criticised Cerularius for presuming to assert his authority over that of his own. Another letter to the Patriarch followed much the same lines and expressed the expectation that Papal authority would be recognised. Upon reception of the envoys, Cerularius rejected their criticisms and even their status as representatives of the Pope, although the Emperor strove to remain courteous and welcoming. At the same time that the party were staying in Constantinople the Pope died. Since they had been his personal representatives, the envoys were thus technically disempowered but the war of words continued, led by Cardinal Humbert of Mourmoutiers who not only exacerbated matters but put forward opinions of his own on the Eastern Church. In the circumstances the Patriarch effectively ignored the Papal legates until Cardinal Humbert and his companions took the unprecedented, and strictly speaking, unlawful step of taking matters into their own hands. The envoys marched into the church of Hagia Sophia on 16 July 1054 AD and, in front of the assembled congregation, placed a document on the altar. The papal ambassadors had drawn up a Bull of Excommunication against the Patriarch of Constantinople. Infuriated, Cerularius had the legates excommunicated. It was a sequence of events that need never have happened and appears to have been, in large measure, based upon personal dislike. All those involved seemed to have behaved like nothing so much as warring wizards of myth hurling spells against one another. Although the papal excommunication was uncanonical and unlawful, it led to a major split between the two churches that was never to be properly resolved.

The Battle of Manzikert

The Battle of Manzikert, fought in 1071, has come to be seen by many historians as marking a pivotal point in the downturn of the fortunes of the Byzantine Empire. John Julius Norwich goes so far as to say that it 'was the greatest disaster suffered by Byzantium in the seven and a half centuries of its existence', (John Julius Norwich, *Byzantium: The Apogee*, p.357). Following the fall of the Armenian capital of Ani to the Seljuk Turks, under the leadership of Alp Arslan, the Byzantine Emperor Romanus IV Diogenes led a force estimated at between 60,000 to 70,000 men against the Turks. In fact, Romanus had agreed a truce with Arslan but the persistent raids by Turkoman tribesmen, acting without the consent of the Sultan, appeared to the Byzantine Emperor to have invalidated it. Interestingly, at the point when Romanus IV decided to march across Anatolia against the Seljuk Turks, Alp Arslan was in the process of moving against the rival Fatimid Caliphate.

Romanus IV sent an envoy to Alp Arslan, offering to give the city of Hierapolis in Syria, captured in 1068, back to the sultan if, in return, the Sultan would restore the Armenian fortresses of Archesh and Manzikert. The appearance of the Byzantine army in Armenia forced Alp Arslan to abandon his projected campaign against the Fatimid Caliphate and assemble an army to meet them in battle. Romanus IV took the decision at Erzurum in Armenia to divide his forces in two and sent the larger part, under the leadership of his general Joseph Tarchaniotes, to capture the fortress of Khelat close to Lake Van. He himself led the remainder of the army against the fortress of Manzikert and captured it without any real difficulties on 23 August 1071.

However, mystery surrounds what happened to the force commanded by Tarchaniotes. Muslim sources claim that he was defeated in battle whilst Byzantine writers say that his army fled from the Seljuk Turks and was not seen again until it arrived at Melitene. It has been conjectured that this was a direct betrayal of the Emperor, aimed at deposing him in favour of his rival Andronicus Ducas.

Based on what little is known, this hypothesis seems the likeliest and, therefore, it was an act of desertion rather than a military defeat that left Romanus IV with his army halved in number. On 24 August, Byzantine foraging parties were attacked by Seljuk forces and the Armenian general Basilacius was sent by Romanus IV against them. However, the strength of the Seljuk troops was greater than the Emperor had anticipated. His general was captured and many of those with him were killed. The Emperor responded by despatching his general Bryennius, with the right wing of the army, against the Seljuks but they were themselves forced back to the Byzantine camp, in all likelihood by the sheer numbers with which they were confronted.

The following day, 25 August, Turkish mercenaries in the service of the Byzantine army deserted and joined the Turkish side. Although this unwelcome development must have been demoralizing to the Byzantine forces, the situation did not seem unrecoverable, particularly when Alp Arslan sent an envoy offering a truce to the camp of the Emperor. However, Romanus IV rejected this offer, apparently either determined to defeat the Turks or unwilling to return home without having properly engaged the enemy.

The battle tactics of the two sides were markedly different. The Byzantine army assembled into a linear formation, prepared for a committed conflict in which one side or the other would finally emerge as victor. The Turks, however, were adept and highly skilled at skirmishing or adopting guerrilla tactics, their archers attacking the enemy on their swift ponies and then fleeing from any real engagements. On 26 August, Romanus IV personally assembled his troops and took command of the central part of the Byzantine line whilst Bryennius took the left side and another general called Alyattes took the right. The Emperor's rival, Andronicus Ducas, commanded the rearguard. As the Byzantine army marched towards the enemy lines, the Turkish troops in the centre gradually fell back whilst the mounted archers harassed the Byzantine troops on either flank. The Turks succeeded in drawing some of the Byzantine cavalry away from the army line and subsequently ambushed them in nearby ravines and difficult country. Finally, realising that they were being drawn further and further from their camp and with the light fading, the Emperor gave the order to head back. At this point confusion seems to have developed amongst the Byzantine army. Some mercenaries thought that the Emperor had been killed and the lines began to disintegrate. Alp Arslan unleashed his full force on the retreating army and managed to separate the Emperor from the protection of the rearguard. It seems likely that Ducas betrayed the Emperor by fleeing the field rather than supporting him and the latter was soon surrounded by the Turks. He made a brave and defiant stand but was overwhelmed and captured.

Romanus IV was brought before Alp Arslan and it seems that the Turkish leader treated his prisoner with great courtesy and respect. He even offered a truce between the two sides and, although he asked for the surrender of several cities, his demands were said to have been surprisingly moderate. The Emperor had little choice but to accept and was personally escorted back by Alp Arslan much of the way to Constantinople. However, if the Sultan had been merciful and magnanimous to Romanus in victory, the same could not be said of the Emperor's treatment on his return to the capital. He was deposed by Michael VII Ducas and, although he was initially promised sanctuary in a monastery if he gave up his title, he was finally blinded and sent to the Island of Proti where he died of his gruesome injuries shortly afterwards.

It was to be the aftermath of the battle that caused the greatest damage to the Byzantine Empire. On seizing the throne Michael VII immediately rejected the truce made with Alp Arslan and effectively goaded the Sultan into taking action several years later. The irony is that the Sultan was, in fact, more concerned with fighting the Fatimid Caliphate than with challenging Byzantium. The political intrigues within Constantinople served only to destabilise the military, particularly the Anatolian themes that provided the army with the majority of its soldiers. Neglecting the maintenance of the Anatolian defences left the way clear for the Turkish forces that, by around 1080, had come to dominate the majority of the former imperial territory in Anatolia. The loss of Anatolia would in turn precipitate the First Crusade when the Emperor Alexius I Comnenus turned to the West for aid in 1095.

The Crusades

The reign of Michael VII (1071–78) was both a troubled and a turbulent time for the Byzantine Empire. The Battle of Manzikert had resulted in the loss of imperial control in the East and the city of Bari, the final stronghold of Byzantine power in Italy, had fallen to the Normans in the same year. Relations with the papacy were dire and the Pecheneg people were creating chaos in the Balkan peninsula. A Norman adventurer called Roussel of Bailleul rebelled against the Emperor and tried to create his own kingdom in Anatolia but failed and was defeated by Byzantine forces. Finally insurrection within Byzantium led to the abdication of Michael VII who was replaced by a nobleman called Nicephorus III Botaneiates. Under this elderly ruler the Empire grew weaker still as Turkish control in Asia Minor became absolute. Nicephorus, in his turn, was forced to abdicate and was sent to a monastery to spend the rest of his life there by the Byzantine general Alexius Comnenus. He was the nephew of former Emperor Isaac Comnenus and was to prove to be an able and effective ruler who would deal with many difficulties and challenges to his empire during his reign.

The first major crisis that faced Alexius took the form of

the Norman warlord Robert Guiscard who had conquered Sicily and much of Southern Italy. A formidable military leader, Robert had been given the epithet of Guiscard, which means 'the Crafty', by his men. Following Guiscard's victories in Southern Italy, the Emperor Michael VII had attempted to reach terms with him by offering to marry his brother to one of the Norman's daughters in exchange for a military treaty. Robert eagerly accepted the offer and it is likely that he had ambitions to sit on the imperial throne himself. Following the successive abdications of Michael VII and Nicephorus III Botaneiates, the agreement was nullified. Having lost this potential bridgehead to the throne, Guiscard simply took the decision to attack the Empire and assembled an army in 1080 AD. His fleet sailed from Italy to Corfu and took the island, offering a point of entry to what is now Albania and the road known as the Via Egnatia that led overland to Constantinople itself. However, Alexius appealed for aid to the Doge of Venice who sent a fleet against the Norman force. For the Venetians, control of the Adriatic was vital to maintain their trade routes. Although the Venetians proved successful against the Norman fleet, the army of Guiscard landed at the town of Durazzo in what is today Albania. Alexius personally led an army against the Normans but Guiscard's troops proved too much for the Byzantine force which was comprised mainly of mercenaries and was diminished in both numbers and effectiveness following the defeat at Manzikert. The Byzantines were beaten back and abandoned the field, finally retreating to Thessalonica. However, Alexius raised funds to instigate a rebellion in Guiscard's Italian lands, forcing him to return to suppress them.

His son Bohemund remained and pursued the campaign and succeeded in conquering territories in Northern Greece. Finally, Alexius inflicted a painful defeat on Bohemund at Larissa in 1083 AD. The Norman army was forced to retreat and Bohemund travelled back to Italy. In his absence the Norman forces either gave up or were overrun. Robert Guiscard launched another offensive against the Empire in 1084 AD and, although its early stages were promising, an outbreak of sickness seriously weakened his force and finally killed him in the following year. The expedition fell apart and, in the short term, the threat of the Normans was ended.

The First Crusade

Although the Normans' ambitions had been temporarily halted, it was not long before new threats to the security of the Empire would emerge. Alexius fought and defeated a Pecheneg army in 1091 with the assistance of a rival tribe called the Cumans. However, the barbarian tribes of Northern Europe remained a constant danger to the Empire and Constantinople was never to be entirely secure from their depredations.

Alexius also had to contend with a Turkish force led by Chaka, the Emir of Smyrna, who had managed to gain substantial control in the Aegean and Eastern Mediterranean seas. He was defeated by a Byzantine naval force close to Constantinople in 1091 AD. Alexius tenaciously fought back all-comers and, when internal bickering between the Turkish leaders in Anatolia began to intensify, it seemed possible that imperial lands might be recaptured. However, the Battle of Manzikert had seriously reduced the forces at the disposal of the Emperor and any military endeavour would require assistance from elsewhere.

In 1094 AD, Pope Urban II invited delegates from Constantinople to attend a council of the Church in the West to be held at Piacenza. Urban had made efforts in the preceding years to reconcile the two churches following the debacle of the Great Schism and the successive problems that had arisen between Rome and Constantinople. For Alexius, it represented an opportunity to further strengthen relations between East and West and also the chance to appeal for military aid in Anatolia. His representatives related the threat posed by the Muslim Turks to Constantinople and, by extension, the danger to the rest of Christian Europe if the Empire should fall. The effect of their speeches was to be profound and dramatic. Pope Urban II called a subsequent council at Clermont in France on 18 November 1095 AD and declared the need for a Holy War in the East. Pope Urban argued that Christians from the West should assist Christians in the East and drew particular attention to the city of Jerusalem. Although the city of Jerusalem had been in Muslim hands for centuries and Christians had largely been tolerated, the current rulers were attacking Christian pilgrims. Pope Urban II called for a Christian army to assemble and embark on a crusade against the Infidel. For some, it was a genuine opportunity to achieve spiritual absolution and visit the Holy Places of Jerusalem. For others, it was a chance to gain land, power and plunder.

The first and quickest response to the Pope's appeal took the form of a Peasants' Crusade, led by an enigmatic figure known as Peter the Hermit. Through a combination of his own personal magnetism and the religious fervour created by the Pope's appeal, Peter gathered a movement that included some knights but was comprised mainly of peasants, both male and female, and that may have numbered as many as 40,000. In Constantinople, the news of the Holy War declared in the West was greeted with alarm and some consternation. Alexius was deeply concerned about the potential damage that an undisciplined army of people Byzantines viewed as barbarians could wreak within the borders of the Empire. The Emperor took immediate steps that would ensure that he was seen to be assisting the crusaders whilst protecting Byzantine interests. Provisions were amassed at points along their route across Greece in an attempt to prevent them looting the local countryside and military police met and escorted crusaders to Constantinople. Peter's army, travelling overland, became involved in violence in the Hungarian city of Belgrade and also at Nish.

However, at Nish, they were suppressed by Byzantine forces who then accompanied them the rest of the way to Constantinople. Alexius showed courtesy and cooperation to the crusaders despite the troubles they had created. Although it was apparent to Alexius that the ill-disciplined army led by Peter stood little chance against the Seljuk Turks in Anatolia, he was keen nonetheless for them to leave Constantinople and had them ferried across to Asia Minor on 6 August 1096 AD. This first people's crusade proved to be a disaster. The various contingents, who all managed to fall out with each other, were successfully overwhelmed by the Turks and were either killed or taken as slaves. By October of 1096 AD the Peasants' Crusade was at an end.

However, the armies that followed this ill-fated expedition from the West were far more formidable and were led by some of the most powerful nobles of Europe.

For the Emperor, this created a series of potential dangers. Firstly, there was the very real possibility that an army of crusaders from the West might actually attempt to overthrow him and capture the Empire for themselves and, secondly, the fear was that they would establish kingdoms for themselves in the Middle East. So, in return for his assistance and cooperation in reaching the Holy Land, he attempted to extract oaths of allegiance from the leaders of the crusade that his authority in the region should be recognised. Some took the oath but others proved more reluctant.

Unlike the ill-equipped and untrained people's army that had preceded them, the crusaders who arrived in Asia Minor in 1097 AD, having travelled via Constantinople, proved to be a success. They took the city of Nicaea in June

1097 AD and defeated the Seljuk Turks at Dorylaeum a month later. The victory at Nicaea restored territory for the Empire but, in most other cases, the crusaders retained the land they captured. In June 1098 AD Antioch was taken and the campaign continued southward. By mid-July 1099 AD, the city of Jerusalem had fallen to the crusaders amidst terrible and violent scenes. The Christian forces killed all the Muslims that resided within the city. The Jewish population, too, was treated mercilessly — forced into the largest synagogue in Jerusalem, which was then set ablaze and burnt to the ground. Whilst the main body of the army had moved onto Jerusalem, Baldwin of Boulogne had struck inland to the desert city of Edessa, which he had succeeded in capturing. He then proclaimed himself Count of Edessa. More disturbingly for the Emperor Alexius, following the capture of Antioch, Bohemund, the son of the Norman adventurer Robert Guiscard, had declared himself to be the Prince of Antioch. He reneged on his oath to return former imperial lands to the Empire and expelled the Greek Patriarch from the city.

In Jerusalem, Godfrey of Lower Lorraine became sovereign, although he refused the title of King in the city where Christ died and was resurrected. Instead he was proclaimed as the 'Defender of the Holy Sepulchre'. Despite his success at Antioch, Bohemund was captured by Danishmend Turks in 1100 and imprisoned for three years. He was finally released after his brother Baldwin, who had by then become King of Jerusalem, paid a ransom for his freedom. Following a series of crusader defeats and hostility between Alexius and Bohemund, the self-proclaimed Prince of Antioch returned to the West to seek support for the new crusader kingdoms.

Bohemund convinced Pope Paschal II that the Byzantine Empire was the enemy of Christendom and he raised an army to attack Constantinople. In 1107 he led a fleet across the Adriatic to Durazzo, intent on its capture. From there, he planned to move overland to Constantinople itself. Alexius himself, supported by mercenaries of the Seljuk Sultan, led an army against him and Bohemund was captured. Alexius forced him to renew his oath of allegiance to him and a peace treaty was agreed. The treaty provided the Empire with a short period of relative peace but, by 1111, it was variously threatened by Turkish attacks and by the ships of the Western trading powers of Genoa and Pisa. Alexius concluded treaties with the Westerners that granted them important trading rights and contained the Turkish attacks. When Alexius died in 1118, his son John II Comnenus succeeded him as Emperor. In 1137, John Comnenus brought the city of Antioch back under imperial control after successive Latin rulers had reneged on their oaths of allegiance. Upon his death in 1143, his son Manuel I Comnenus became Emperor.

When the Muslim forces of Imad ed-Din Zengi captured the County of Edessa in 1145, the situation in the crusader state of Outremer led to calls for a Second Crusade. The initial wave of enthusiasm that had accompanied the success of the First Crusade had faded and, as was to be the case throughout the history of the Latin Kingdoms in the East, manpower was now urgently needed. Bernard, the Abbot of Clairvaux, was to be instrumental in raising support for a Second Crusade that was led by King Louis VII of France and King Conrad III of Germany. It was to prove a disaster and ended in a humiliating defeat in 1148 at the hands of forces of Nur ed-Din, the son of Zengi. However, internal disputes within the Islamic forces prevented a concerted effort against the Crusader Kingdoms in the East until the emergence of Saladin as a unifying leader in the 1170s.

The death of Manuel I Comnenus in 1180 precipitated a dark and troubled episode in the history of Byzantium. Manuel had been fascinated by the culture and customs of Western Europe and had married a Latin, Mary of Antioch. Although his son, Alexius II Comnenus, was named as his successor, he was still a child and his mother ruled as Regent in his stead. This created great resentment in Constantinople where many were appalled that a foreign barbarian should hold so much power and feared an increase in Western influence on the Empire. The first cousin of the young Emperor, Andronicus Comnenus, capitalised on the unpopularity of Mary of Antioch and staged a coup, supported by the people of Constantinople. It was to be a bloody and vicious insurrection that would set the tone for his subsequent reign and earn him the epithet of Andronicus the Terrible. The young Emperor and his mother were imprisoned and then killed and a terrible massacre of the Latin population of Constantinople followed. Andronicus became Emperor in 1183 but he soon faced a major invasion by Norman Sicilian forces who captured the strategically important harbour of Durazzo in 1185. Within the Empire, Andronicus began a sadistic campaign of violence against what he saw as corruption within the state that would change his popular status from saviour to tyrant. The Sicilian army then marched on Thessalonica, which Andronicus had ordered to be prepared for the oncoming assault, but, through the incompetence of its Governor, it fell to the invaders. The sack of Thessalonica, with the slaughter of its citizens and the profanation of its Holy Places, was particularly shocking. As many as 8,000 people are claimed to have been killed by the Normans before order was restored. The Norman army then marched on Constantinople.

In the face of this catastrophe the people of Constantinople rebelled against Andronicus and his cousin Isaac Angelus was crowned Emperor. Andronicus failed to oppose the coup effectively and was subsequently handed to the people who killed him. Isaac mobilised all the troops at his disposal and inflicted a crushing defeat on the Normans. When the news of the defeat of the main Norman army reached Thessalonica, the people of the city overwhelmed the garrison and the remaining Norman survivors. Isaac had succeeded in averting disaster at a time of crisis – a triumph that in many ways typifies the spirit and character of the Byzantine Empire – but, as always, new threats would emerge in the near future.

The Fall of Jerusalem to Saladin in 1187 led to calls for a Third Crusade to be led by Frederick Barbarossa. Isaac

Angelus greatly feared that Barbarossa would attempt to overrun Constantinople en route to the Middle East but he agreed to assist in the transportation of the crusaders as long as they stayed clear of the capital. Barbarossa died in 1190 in Asia Minor, either drowning or suffering a heart attack when crossing a river, and his death lessened Isaac's worries. Although the Third Crusade did not succeed in its goal of capturing Jerusalem, the armies of Richard the Lionheart and Philip Augustus of France ensured the short-term survival of the remaining, diminished crusader kingdoms. In 1195 Isaac Angelus was overthrown by Alexius III, his older brother. According to Byzantine custom, he was blinded so that he could not regain the throne.

The Fourth Crusade

Innocent III became pope in 1198 and wasted no time in calling for a new crusade. Its initial target was to be Egypt which Richard the Lionheart had believed was the most vulnerable part of the East to attack. During this period, Europe was in turmoil following the death of Richard and internal strife in Germany. However, for this crusade, Innocent III hoped to exert a greater papal control of the crusader armies and he appointed Count Tibald of Champagne as its leader. In order to attack the infidel through Egypt, the crusaders needed to assemble a substantial fleet to carry them to their destination. Innocent turned to the Republic of Venice to fulfil this purpose and he dispatched a party of six representatives to the city to discuss matters with the Venetians in 1201. For the substantial sum of 84,000 silver marks, Doge Enrico Dandolo agreed to ship the crusader army to Egypt and to supply 50 galleys from the Republic itself. In addition, the Doge negotiated an agreement that the Republic should be given half of any lands taken during the expedition. However, when the army assembled in 1202, only a third of those expected to fight arrived in Venice. For many, the decision to attack through Egypt was unpopular since Jerusalem itself was seen as the central goal of any crusade. This created the immediate problem that insufficient funds were collected by the crusader army to pay the Doge for his transport. At this point, following the death of Tibald, Marquis Boniface of Montferrat was in control of the army. As an alternative form of payment the Doge suggested that the crusaders should supply him with military assistance in recapturing Zara on the Adriatic coast, a city that had belonged to the Venetians but had been taken by the King of Hungary. Many were appalled by this idea, as the King of Hungary was a Christian who had been on crusade himself. However, the proposal was finally accepted and the fleet set off from Venice later that year. It succeeded in capturing Zara but Pope Innocent III was so infuriated by the attack that he excommunicated the entire crusader army. He later relented towards the crusaders, although the Doge and his followers remained excommunicates.

Whilst the crusaders were based at Zara, the son of Isaac Angleus, the Byzantine Emperor who had been overthrown and blinded by his own brother Alexius III, arrived seeking aid in regaining the throne. In return for military assistance, the son of Isaac, another Alexius, offered substantial financial rewards, a promise of soldiers for the campaign in Egypt and, even more dramatically, that the Eastern Church would recognise the supremacy of the papacy. The offer was readily accepted, under the rather flimsy premise that it would unify Christendom, although, in reality, its appeal for the majority of the crusaders was that it offered material rewards and significant booty. The crusader fleet arrived at Constantinople in 1203 and captured the suburb of Galata. They attacked the city, whose inhabitants were amazed by the turn of events, but were thrown back by the Varangian guard loyal to the Emperor Alexius III. However, despite the failure of the attack, Alexius III panicked and fled Constantinople.

The decision was taken by court officials to re-institute the deposed Emperor and he made his son Alexius co-Emperor. The agreement they then made led to bitter hatred towards the crusaders within Constantinople and, in January 1204, Isaac and Alexius were deposed. They were replaced by Alexius V Ducas Murzuphlus who refused to meet the crusaders' terms. The crusaders then decided to attack the city and they eventually succeeded in gaining access to Constantinople and letting in the Western army. Once again the Emperor deserted Constantinople and the city was sacked.

The Byzantine chronicler Nicholas Mesarites describes an almost apocalyptic scene, 'war-maddened swordsmen, breathing murder, iron-clad and spear-bearing, sword-bearers and lance bearers, bowmen, horsemen, boasting dreadfully, baying like Cerebus and breathing like Charon, pillaging the holy places, trampling on divine things, casting down to the floor the holy images (on walls or panels) of Christ and His holy Mother and of the holy men who from eternity have been pleasing to the Lord God'. (Quoted in Jonathan Phillips, *The Fourth Crusade and the Sack of Constantinople*, p.259).

For three days the crusaders ran riot, pillaging, killing and raping the inhabitants of Constantinople. Count Baldwin of Flanders and Hainault was made Emperor and the Empire was divided amongst the crusaders, with the Venetians under Doge Dandolo benefitting most.

The Latin Empire

In the aftermath of the fall and sack of Constantinople, a new political landscape emerged from the former Byzantine territories. The new Emperor, Baldwin I, had been chosen by the Venetians as a malleable and controllable figure and he ruled an empire vastly reduced in size. He was given Thrace, a handful of islands in the Aegean Sea and territories in north-west Asia Minor. The former leader of the crusaders, Boniface of Montferrat, set up the Kingdom of Thessalonica. William de Champlitte was appointed the Prince of Achaea and Otto de la Roche became the Duke of Athens.

The Venetians took over many of the most profitable and productive territories in the Aegean as well as parts of the

Adriatic coast and, notably, Crete. The overall effect of these states was to create a patchwork of power.

The Empire of Nicaea

Most surprisingly of all in the circumstances was that a number of large Byzantine controlled territories were to survive the fall of Constantinople. The so-called Despotate of Epirus was one of these Byzantine states and another was the Empire of Trebizond on the Black Sea Coast of Asia Minor. The most significant and important of all was the Empire of Nicaea that occupied a substantial section of Western and Central Anatolia. Baldwin I was to last only a year as Emperor before he was defeated in battle and taken prisoner by Tsar Kalojan of Bulgaria who hoped to take the throne with Greek support in Thrace. Baldwin I was succeeded by his brother, Henry of Hainault, who attempted to suppress the Empire of Nicaea but, harried by Bulgars, was forced to seek a treaty with its ruler, Theodore I Lascaris, in 1214. In 1222, John Vatatzes became Emperor of Nicaea following Theodore I Lascaris, his father-in-law. Arguably, Vatatzes was to do more than any other single individual towards regaining Constantinople for the exiled Byzantines. Henry of Hainault was succeeded as the Latin Emperor of Constantinople by his brother-in-law Peter of Courtenay in 1217 but Peter was captured on campaign against the Despot of Epirus and rapidly replaced by his wife Yolanda. When her son, Robert of Courtenay, proved to be a hopelessly ineffective ruler and was defeated in battle by Vatatzes, the crusader barons of Constantinople turned to John of Brienne who had been the King of Jerusalem. Robert's younger brother Baldwin II was still a boy at the time of his accession to the throne in 1228 and Brienne was to rule until he reached adulthood.

Michael Palaeologus

When John Vatatzes died in 1254, his son Theodore II Lascaris inherited the Empire of Nicaea. Although he proved to be an able ruler, it was to be a talented young general in his service called Michael Palaeologus who would finally reclaim Constantinople from the Latin Emperors and be declared Basileus by the Byzantines. Michael was of an aristocratic Byzantine background with links to the Angelus, Comneneus and Ducas families which had all produced Emperors that had ruled from Constantinople. When Theodore II Lascaris died in 1258, after a lifetime of suffering from epilepsy, his son was still only a child and he named George Muzalon as his successor. Michael was passed over by Theodore, who had known and hated him since they were children, but a plot was hatched. Muzalon was murdered and Michael acclaimed in his stead. In 1261, a Byzantine force led by the Caesar Alexius Strategopulus succeeded in making its way in secret into Constantinople. The Latin Emperor Baldwin II, finding the enemy army in the city, fled almost instantly to the island of Euboea. The remaining Franks and Venetians evacuated the city and, on 15 August 1261, Michael VIII

Palaeologus was again crowned Emperor, this time in the church of St Sophia by the patriarch of Constantinople, Arsenius.

The Siege of Constantinople

Although the Byzantines under Michael Palaeologus had succeeded in recapturing Constantinople, the Empire itself had been shattered forever. Its once great territories had been reduced to what amounted to fragments of Byzantine power such as the Empire of Trebizond on the Black Sea coast. In truth, the Emperors who now ruled from Constantinople were no more powerful than the various princes, potentates and warlords who had carved out kingdoms for themselves in former imperial territories.

The next two centuries would see the rapid growth in power of the Ottoman Turks in Anatolia who expanded to the point where Constantinople was effectively surrounded by territories controlled by them. Under the Sultan Murad I, the Ottomans dominated much of Greece. In 1387, Thessalonica surrendered to his forces. His son Bayezit succeeded him in 1389 and, in 1402, he marched against Constantinople, demanding that the Emperor Manuel II Palaeologus surrender the city to him. Manuel was travelling in Western Europe, trying with little success to secure aid for his beleaguered empire, when the ultimatum was delivered. However, Constantinople was saved when the forces of Timur the Tartar attacked the Turks and Bayezit was compelled to withdraw to face them.

In the next few decades, Constantinople was given a reprieve because of the infighting between the Turks. When the Sultan Murad II marched on Constantinople in 1423, his plans had to be abandoned so that he could deal with the threat of rebellion. In later years, Murad would largely maintain his territories rather than seek to expand them. For many Greek Byzantines his death was noted with some sadness not least because his son and successor Mehmet II, who came to power in 1452, was thought to be altogether less tolerant to the existence of Constantinople. When Manuel II Palaeologus died in 1425 he was succeeded by his eldest son John VIII Palaeologus. John VIII attempted to secure Western Aid by agreeing to a union of the Orthodox and the Catholic Churches at the council of Florence in 1439. However, it was to prove extremely unpopular in Constantinople. He died in 1448 without an heir and he therefore nominated his brother Constantine XI Palaeologus, supported by their mother, the Empress Helena, to succeed him.

Rumeli Hisar Fortress

In 1452 Mehmet took the decision to build a fortress on the European side of the Bosphorus opposite Anadolu Hisar, the castle that his great-grandfather Bayezit had built on the shores of Asia Minor. It would be sited to the north of Constantinople and be of major strategic value in controlling the Bosphorus and, in particular, entry for ships travelling either to or from the Black Sea. The Christian Genoese colonies strung along the Black Sea coast would be then unable to offer assistance to Constantinople. Anadolu was the name given to the Asian part of the Ottoman Empire whilst Rumeli indicated the European territory. The land on which Mehmet intended to build his new fortress belonged to the Byzantine Empire and, on hearing of the Sultan's intentions, Constantine XI protested that his great-grandfather Bayezit had first consulted with the Emperor before building his fortress.

Constantine attempted to sway the young sultan with presents and asked that Byzantine villages nearby should be unharmed. His concerns and requests were ignored and, finally, when he sent ambassadors asking that the Sultan state that the building of the fortress was not intended to assist in an attack on Constantinople, they were seized and beheaded. Mehmet had made his position frighteningly clear to the Emperor. The castle was originally known in Turkish as 'Boghaz-kesen', a term that meant both 'the strait cutter' and 'the throat-cutter', illustrating its specific military value and its proposed use.

Rumeli Hisar was built between April and August 1452 at astonishing speed and it is still in existence today. A huge structure, it was equipped with three large cannons aimed across the Bosphorus. Mehmet lost no time in issuing an order that all ships passing the castle must halt and allow an inspection to be carried out by the Sultan's men. At first the demand was ignored. Two Venetian ships, travelling from ports on the Black Sea in November, avoided fire from the

cannon and escaped examination. However, shortly afterwards, another Venetian ship on its way to Constantinople
was attacked and sunk in the straits. Its captain, Antonio
Rizzo, and his crew were captured. Mehmet ordered the
immediate execution of the crew whilst Rizzo was impaled
by a nearby road, as a warning to anyone who dared to
challenge the authority of the Sultan.

Reactions amongst the Venetians and Genoese were
mixed. Although appalled by the fate of the unfortunate
Rizzo, many in Venice were concerned to maintain good
links with the Sultan because they traded with Ottoman
territories. At the same time the Venetians traded profitably
with Constantinople where a Venetian quarter had long
been established. It was decided that Venetians should adopt
the difficult policy of helping their fellow Christians in
Constantinople but without engaging in hostilities with the
Turks. The Genoese, who inhabited the colony of Pera (also
known as Galata) across the waters of the Golden Horn
opposite Constantinople, were caught in a similar predicament. Whilst some Genoese opted to aid the Byzantine
Emperor in the event of hostilities the leader or Podesta of
Pera, ultimately putting Genoese commercial concerns
first, sought to effect a strategy of neutrality.

Constantine appealed to Pope Nicholas for aid and
agreed to enact the union of the Eastern and Western
Churches that had been agreed at the Council of Florence
in 1439. The Pope was sympathetic to the plight of the
Emperor and tried to raise support for Byzantium but with
little success. Nonetheless, in 1452, Cardinal Isidore, a

former Metropolitan of Kiev, was despatched to Constantinople by the Pope to bring about the union between Catholics and Orthodox Christians. With him came two hundred archers from Naples, paid for by the Pope himself. The move towards a union of the Churches had been opposed by many in the city, led by a man called George Scholarius, who had taken the name of Gennadius on becoming a monk. The sinking of the Venetian ship and the murder of its captain, Antonio Rizzo, swayed public opinion in favour of the union with the hope of Western military aid it brought. A service took place on 12 December 1452 in the church of St Sophia, in which the union of East and West was proclaimed, but popular reaction amongst the Byzantines was muted and most, shunning the pro-unionist churches, preferred to worship in churches where the orthodox liturgy continued.

In January 1453, Mehmet called an assembly of his ministers at Adrianople. During the course of the meeting he argued that the security of the Ottoman Empire was threatened by the continuing presence of Constantinople in its midst. Whilst the Byzantine Empire had been whittled away to a fraction of its former size, the capital still posed a potential danger, particularly if they were to receive support from Christians in Western Europe. Constantinople must therefore be conquered by the Ottoman Empire and its Emperor deposed. The city was formidably defended, possessing probably the most significant fortifications in the medieval world, and previous attempts to take Constantinople had failed largely because of the inability of aggressors to control the sea approaches. Now that the Turks had gained a considerable hold of the waters surrounding Constantinople, it would be possible to starve out its inhabitants through a protracted siege if military might alone proved insufficient. War was declared against Byzantium.

Preparations for the Siege of Constantinople

In the build-up to an assault on Constantinople those towns still controlled by the Emperor in Thrace were attacked and overwhelmed by the Turks. Meanwhile, the Byzantine presence in the Peloponnese, based around the fortress of Mystras, was kept pinned down by Turkish forces so that it was unable to send help to the Emperor. In March 1453, Mehmet also gave instructions for a great Turkish fleet to be created and gathered near to Gallipoli. In the past, Christian nations had possessed better ships and sailors that the Turks had themselves used for transportation in return for payment. Now, however, the Sultan aimed to maintain control over the sea and consequently over supplies to and from Constantinople. From contemporary sources it is thought that the Turkish fleet contained ten biremes, boats with single sails and paired banks of rowers, six triremes, double-masted crafts with rowers grouped in threes, and fifteen oared galleys. There were numerous smaller craft including 75 fustae, a type of long boat, and 20 heavy sailing barges known as parandaria. It is likely other vessels were also involved, creating a formidable Turkish naval presence. Suleiman Baltoghlu, who was the governor of Gallipoli, led this navy.

Estimates of the scale of the army that Mehmet led into Thrace at the same time vary wildly. Some claim as many as 300,000 to 400,000 but a figure closer to 100,000, still impressive, is more likely. The army was formed of around 80,000 Ottoman troops plus 20,000 Bashi-bazouks who were a mixture of Christian and Muslim men of many races who lacked the training and the equipment of the main army but who could provide a ferocious first wave of attack. The Sultan took greatest pride in his regiment of Janissaries. These soldiers were taken from Christian families whilst children and raised as fiercely devout Muslims. Provided with intensive military training, they combined military discipline with a fanatic devotion to Islam.

Whilst the Sultan was able to assemble a huge army and fleet, perhaps his most significant weapon was to prove to be the cannons that he had made to attack Constantinople. Significantly, in 1452, a Hungarian engineer called Urban had approached the Emperor Constantine XI, offering his skills as an artillery specialist.

Sadly and, as it was to prove, ironically, the Emperor was unable to afford his services and so Urban promptly approached the Sultan instead. Mehmet was delighted when Urban announced that he could create a cannon that would 'blast the walls of Babylon itself'. It was Urban who supplied the great cannon of Rumeli Hisar. Impressed, Mehmet ordered the creation of an even greater cannon that is thought to have measured twenty-six feet and eight inches (over eight metres) in length. Capable of propelling a cannonball weighing twelve hundredweight (544 kg) a distance of a mile, it was an awesome weapon for its time.

The city of Constantinople was well served by its incredible fortifications, defended as it was by walls which were fourteen miles in length and were formed of a sequence of floodable ditches, outer walls and inner walls. However, the Byzantines were desperately short of manpower. When Constantine gave his secretary Sphrantzes the order to carry out a census of defenders that the city could muster, the results horrified him. Around 5,000 Greeks could be called upon, supplemented by about 2,000 foreign personnel. Sphrantzes was ordered to keep this a secret for fear that the defenders would despair and flee. The Byzantine forces were supported by the Venetians who lived in the city with some reinforcements from Crete, then a Venetian colony.

Although the government of Genoa had not sent aid to Constantinople a group of Genoese led by Giovanni Giustiniani Longo sailed to the city in January 1453.

These Genoese brought with them an engineer called Johannes Grant who is thought to have been Scottish and who would prove to be of great help to the Emperor and his people. The defenders also included a group of Catalans led by their elderly but gallant Don, Francisco de Toledo.

The Siege of Constantinople

The Sultan's army arrived at the walls of Constantinople on Easter Monday, 2 April 1453. On sighting the enemy,

Constantine gave the order to close and secure all the city gates and a great chain or boom was stretched across the harbour of the Golden Horn, attached at its opposite end to a tower in the Genoese suburb of Galata. On 6 April, the Sultan offered the Emperor and the citizens the chance to surrender in accordance with Islamic law under which their lives and possessions would be spared. The Byzantines stood firm, knowing that, as a result, no quarter would now be given. The Emperor and Giustiniani took control of the defence of what was thought to be the section of the walls most susceptible to attack. Called the *mesoteichion*, it was here that the river Lycus flowed into the city via a culvert. An artillery bombardment began against the walls but this was hampered by the slow rate of reloading of the cannon. The Byzantines worked furiously to repair the damaged sections of walls and the Turks were fought off when they tried to capitalise on damage done by the cannon. Attempts to destroy the great harbour chain across the Golden Horn also proved unsuccessful and the Christian ships, in part because they were taller, were able to attack the Turkish fleet effectively. The elevation of the cannon of the Turks proved insufficient to do them real damage whilst the Venetians and Genoese could also boast superior seamanship amongst their crews. On 20 April, three ships sent with provisions by the Pope, accompanied by a Byzantine vessel, arrived in the Sea of Marmara. The Turkish fleet blockading the city had turned its attentions away from incoming vessels and the element of surprise allowed the Christian vessels to approach the city. They were soon surrounded and a desperate battle began between the Christian and Turkish crews.

Although outnumbered, the Christian ships had both the advantage of height and experienced crews and the Byzantine vessel was able to make good use of its stocks of Greek fire. At one point the vessels adopted the tactic of lashing their ships together to smash their way through the Turkish fleet. Events were watched from the shore by the Sultan himself who reportedly rode excitedly into the sea to urge on his men. Finally, with a strong wind behind them, the Christian vessels were able to break through the blockade and enter the Golden Horn. The Sultan was furious and nearly had his naval commander Baltoghlu executed. He was only saved from death by the intervention of other naval officers. In the event, he was stripped of his command and possessions which were handed out to the Janissaries.

The problem of breaking the sea chain that protected the Golden Horn greatly perplexed the Sultan. The difficulty of bringing Turkish ships into the Golden Horn posed a great challenge but a startling and ingenious solution was hit upon. Mehmet ordered that Turkish ships and boats be transported overland from the Bosphorous across a high ridge. A road was built and the ships carried on cradles pulled by teams of oxen. The Byzantines were horrified by this turn of events and morale was badly hit when an attempt to destroy the Turkish fleet now in the Golden Horn was foiled. Although the Turks were so far unable to overwhelm the defence the stranglehold on the city meant that supplies were growing short and tensions developed between the defenders. The Genoese at Pera who remained neutral drew particular criticism. The Emperor appealed for unity and succeeded in calming the situation to some extent. It is thought that the Emperor attempted to open talks with the Sultan in late April. Mehmet remained unmoved, stating only that if the city surrendered its people would be spared and Constantine would be allowed to leave for the Byzantine stronghold of the Morea in the Peloponnese. The Emperor refused to abandon the city and its people even if it meant the chance of regrouping Byzantine forces whilst in exile.

The Turks tried to beat the stalemate by mining under the city walls. However, the Scottish engineer Johannes Grant created counter tunnels that gave the Byzantines the chance to kill or capture the Turks undermining the city defences. By capturing an important Turkish sapper, the Byzantines gained vital information about the remaining tunnels and they were destroyed. On 3 May, a Venetian ship had managed to escape from Constantinople to search for any relief vessels from the West, disguised as a Turkish ship. However, on 23 May, it returned to the city with the terrible news that no ships had been sighted or even heard of in the Aegean. The crew themselves had voted to return to inform the Emperor even though it put their own lives at risk. When the Emperor met the men personally he is said to have wept as he expressed his gratitude for their loyalty. The fate of the city, it now seemed, lay in the hands of God.

As the defenders struggled with the pressures of a

protracted siege, a series of what seemed to be ill omens further underlined the apparent hopelessness of the situation.

An eclipse of the moon on 22 May, when the moon was full, disquieted the people of Constantinople, recalling an ancient prophecy that the city would fall when the moon was waning. Popular belief also held that just as the first Emperor of Constantinople was called Constantine, whose mother was named Helena, so the current Emperor Constantine XI, son of Empress Helena, would be the last.

Perhaps more troubling still, when the people were carrying the holiest and most revered icon of the Mother of God through the streets in one final desperate call for divine assistance, the image fell from the platform upon which it had been placed.

It is said that, when attempts were made to lift the Icon of the Virgin, it became suddenly and supernaturally heavy and it was only after some struggle that it was reinstated in the procession. As the supplicants marched onwards, a sudden and terrible thunderstorm struck the city and the rain and hail became so intense that the procession was forced to end. So violent was the storm that streets were flooded and children had to be rescued by their parents. The portents of destruction seemed to continue the following day when the people of Constantinople awoke to find that a thick and enveloping fog covered the city, a highly unusual and unprecedented event at that time of year. Both Muslims and Christians looked with a mixture of wonder, fear and awe when, that night, a mysterious light appeared around the dome of the church of St Sophia and was extinguished just as suddenly as it had appeared. The Sultan himself was greatly unnerved by the light but was reassured by his spiritual advisors that it was a sign that the light of the True Faith would illuminate the great church. For the Byzantines, it was a confirmation that the Divine Spirit had left the city. It was also said that watchmen on the towers of the city walls saw mysterious lights in the far distance and some took heart, believing that it was the lights of an approaching army come to rescue them. However, the defenders were now alone.

Constantine's ministers attempted to persuade the Emperor to flee the city to lead a resistance movement in exile in the Peloponnese. It is reported that the Emperor was so exhausted by the struggle that, as they implored him to go, he fainted. When he came round his resolve was unaffected – he would stay and fight for his city and his people even if it meant his own death.

The Fall of Constantinople

The frustration of the Sultan at the failure of the siege to take the city led him to plan a final decisive attack. Rightly, he believed that the defenders were exhausted and that they could be overcome by sheer weight of numbers. He announced his attentions to his court on Saturday 26 May, although, interestingly, his Grand Vizier Halil Pasha opposed the plan and thought his master, who was aged only twenty-one, had been foolish to attack the city in the first place. But Mehmet was determined and overruled him. It was decided that Sunday would be spent organising the final assault whilst Monday would be given over to rest and prayer. The attack would take place on Tuesday 29 May. News of the planned assault reached Constantinople as Christians on the Turkish side fired arrows into the city with messages attached to them. Within Constantinople, on Monday 28 May, a final procession was held, joined by Genoese, Venetians and Byzantines in an intermingling of Orthodox and Catholic traditions. The Emperor is said to have assembled his commanders and personally thanked them and asked that they might forgive him any offence he had ever given them. The defenders took their positions along the walls whilst the Emperor spent the evening in prayer before making a final circuit of the defences. Accompanied by his secretary George Sphrantzes, he climbed a tower to look out at the Turkish army and stayed for around an hour. When the two men left, it was to be a final farewell for both of them.

The assault was launched in the early hours of the morning and the Sultan unleashed a wave of Bashi-bazouks against the city walls focusing particularly around the section where the river Lycus ran into the city. They were repelled but the Sultan planned to weary the defenders with successive waves of attack. The second attack consisted of Anatolian troops and came close to breaching the walls but they were again thrown back by the defenders, led by the Emperor. A third wave was formed of the Sultan's favoured Janissaries. With some difficulty the defenders managed to contain even them. However, at this point, two events occurred that changed the balance of the conflict in favour of the Turks. The Genoese general Giovanni Giustiniani was injured during the fighting and, in great pain, asked to be taken for medical help. The Emperor implored him to stay, fearing that, with the departure of their leader who had fought bravely and tenaciously, the Genoese men might flee the battle. The Emperor was right. As soon as Giovanni Giustiniani was carried away, his men panicked and followed him. The Turks capitalised on this setback and pressed home the attack, pushing the defenders back to the inner wall. Not long afterwards, a group of Turks succeeded in raising their flag on the city walls, after discovering that a small door known as the Kerkoporta had been left open. More and more Turkish troops rushed in, overwhelming the defenders. The Emperor himself was last seen throwing off his imperial insignia and rushing into the thick of the fighting with his cousin and friend and with the loyal Catalan grandee Don Francisco de Toledo.

Before the final assault the Sultan had promised his troops that they could loot and pillage the city for three days following its conquest. However, such was the ferocity and violence of the troops as they slaughtered, raped or enslaved the population that Mehmet called an end to their activities after only one day, probably because he saw public buildings being damaged. When the city was secured, Mehmet entered in a procession hailing him as the conquering victor. Before entering the church of St Sophia he is said to have sprinkled earth on his turban as a sign of humility before God. Mehmet ordered that the ancient Christian church be converted to a mosque and an imam climbed into the pulpit and declared that there was no God but Allah and Mohammed was his Prophet.

The Shadow of Empire

For Mehmet, the conquest of Constantinople did not simply represent the taking of a great city. The Byzantine Empire that had developed from the Eastern half of the Roman Empire had begun with the decision of Constantine the Great to make Constantinople its capital. The city was dedicated on Monday 11 May 330 AD, and had survived until Tuesday 29 May 1453. During the 1123 years and 18 days of its existence the Byzantine Empire had been a superpower of the ancient world that had survived innumerable wars, upheavals and difficulties, not least of which was the final fall of the Western Roman Empire in 476 AD. Although its power and prestige had declined steadily over the intervening centuries until finally Constantinople had, in many ways, come to represent, in effect, the surviving head of the lost body of Empire, something of the glory of its famous past survived even until the end. As Mehmet the 'Conqueror of Byzantium', the Sultan saw himself as the direct successor of the Roman Emperors, a viewpoint borne out by his decision to make Constantinople the capital of the Ottoman Empire. However, Mehmet was now in possession of a city that had been badly damaged during the struggle to take it and which, in previous years, had been undermined by the decay and depopulation following its capture during the Fourth Crusade.

In the aftermath of the capture of the city, mystery surrounded the final fate of Constantine XI, the Last Emperor of Byzantium. It seems most likely, particularly given the evidence of the Emperor's secretary George Sphrantzes, that Constantine was killed during the fighting. The former Metropolitan of Kiev, Cardinal Isidore, who had travelled to Constantinople to implement the union of the Churches, survived the siege and claimed that the body of the Emperor had been identified after the fighting and Turkish soldiers had cut off the head and presented it in triumph to the Sultan. According to the renowned crusades historian Steven Runciman, 'A story was circulated later round the Italian colonies in the Levant that two Turkish soldiers who claimed to have killed Constantine brought a head to the Sultan which captured courtiers who were present recognised as their master's. Mehmet set it for a while on a column in the Augustean Forum, then stuffed it and sent it to be exhibited round the leading courts of the Islamic World', (Steven Runciman, *The Fall of Constantinople 1453*, p143).

Another story, a version of which was recorded by Makaris Melissenos in the sixteenth century, claims that George Sphrantzes discovered that the Sultan had ordered that a search be made for the body of the Emperor. It was finally recognised by Turkish soldiers when they found a body wearing greaves stamped with the insignia of the Imperial Eagle. According to Melissenos, the Sultan decreed that the body of the Emperor should be given a Christian burial but this seems unlikely and is largely dismissed by historians. Numerous myths and legends about the final resting place of the last Byzantine Emperor were to spring up over the following centuries and various locations within the city itself have been suggested as the spot. More prosaically, it may be that the body of the Emperor was buried with those of the other soldiers who died defending Constantinople in an unmarked grave.

Greek Orthodox Church

Whilst the Sultan saw himself as the successor to the Emperors of Byzantium and was referred to as 'Kayser-i-Rum', Emperor of the Romans, he decided that the citizens of Constantinople would be allowed to practice their faith. The Byzantines left in the city would be self-governing with the Sultan as their overlord. As so many of the aristocratic families had either been killed during the siege or had fled the city, many taking refuge in the Greek islands or Italy, particularly in Venice, the patriarch of the Orthodox Church would become their leader. Although the Orthodox Church had technically undergone union with the Catholic Church before the siege, public opinion now rejected it. The most recent patriarch had been Gregory III but he had resigned from his post and left Constantinople for Italy. Gregory had been in favour of union between the Churches and therefore Mehmet was unwilling to recall him, even if he had wanted to return, on the grounds that it might lead to the papacy offering military aid against the Ottoman Empire in the future. The Sultan therefore decided to appoint George Scholarius who had originally been in favour of union but had finally rejected it and led the movement in favour of the independence of the Orthodox Church. Scholarius had taken the name Gennadius on becoming a monk and, after the fall of Constantinople, had been taken into slavery by a wealthy Turk who lived in the Anatolian city of Adrianople. Mehmet freed him from his enslavement and elevated him to the position of Patriarch. Traditionally, the Patriarch underwent his ceremonial appointment at the Church of Hagia Sophia but, as this great masterpiece of Byzantine culture had been transformed into a mosque, the ceremony took place at the Church of the Holy Apostles in January 1454. The Sultan himself assumed the role of Emperor and presented Scholarius with his symbols of power. Although the Orthodox were allowed to worship as they chose, when Scholarius voluntarily changed its headquarters, the Church of the Holy Apostles was destroyed and a mosque built in its stead. The new headquarters of the Church became Theotokos Pammakaristos. However, the location of the Patriarchal See was to change again and finally settled on the Golden Horn in the Fener quarter. Today the Patriachate of Constantinople is still considered to be the 'Mother Church' of Greece. Of the 81 dioceses of the Church of Greece, 30 remain at least nominally under the jurisdiction of Constantinople. The Patriarchate of Constantinople has a recognised jurisdiction over the islands of the Dodecanese, Crete and the monastic communities of Mount Athos.

It has been claimed that, as well as viewing themselves as the natural successors to the Roman Emperors, the Ottomans also adopted the flag of Byzantium as their own after conquering Constantinople. It is said that, in 670 BC, when Byzantium was a Greek city state, its inhabitants made the crescent moon their symbol following an important victory in battle. They believed that they had won this victory with the help of Artemis, Goddess of the Hunt who was associated with this image. It is interesting to note that, in pre-Christian times, the city was viewed as being under the protection of a goddess and that, during the Christian era, it was believed that Constantinople enjoyed the protection and favour of the Mother of God, the Blessed Virgin. The crescent moon was joined by the sign of the star, a symbol associated with the Virgin, when Constantine the Great combined the two on the flag of Byzantium in 330 AD. It has been argued that the Turkish flag featuring the star and crescent derives from the flag of Byzantium itself.

The Despotate of Morea and the Empire of Trebizond

Although the fall of Constantinople effectively marked the end of the Empire, two remaining Byzantine territories outlived its celebrated capital for a brief time. The Despots of the Morea in the Peloponese, Thomas and Demetrius, brothers of the last Emperor, Constantine XI Palaeologus, attempted to bargain with the Sultan but were finally over-whelmed by the Ottomans in 1460. The Empire of Trebizond, on the coast of the Black Sea, came to an end on 15 August 1461 when the Emperor David Comnenus capit-ulated to Mehmet. The fall of Constantinople was also to have a profound and dramatic effect on the powerful Western city-states of Venice and Genoa. Although Venetians and Genoese had fought alongside the defenders of the city, attempts were made in the aftermath of the Ottoman victory to forge diplomatic relations with the Sultan. To that end, ambassadors were dispatched to the court of Mehmet to try to re-establish terms for the continuation of trading in the East.

The Sultan, however, remained largely unmoved by the gifts that he received during these negotiations and neither the Genoese or Venetians were able to secure particularly favourable terms. It was agreed that the Venetians might retain a settlement within the city of Constantinople but without the privileges that had brought it economic success under Byzantine rulers. The Genoese were also allowed to retain their settlement at Galata but they were required to demolish the walls of the town and, although they were allowed to worship as Christians, they were ordered to refrain from ringing church bells. However, the real blow to the Genoese was the huge charges that the Sultan imposed on their merchant ships to travel to the trading ports of the Black Sea. As a result of this effective strangle-hold the power and influence of both these maritime powers were drastically reduced.

The Silk Road

For centuries, Constantinople had served as the major route between Europe and Asia and was an important city on the ancient Silk Road. Many merchants and explorers had passed through the city in its long history including Marco Polo and the Islamic traveller Ibn Battuta. Marco Polo had lived in the Venetian quarter of Constantinople in 1259, during the period of Latin Rule, but left shortly before the Byzantine Emperor Michael Palaeologus reclaimed the city in 1261. Polo travelled eastwards to the Black Sea and followed the Silk Road to China where he claimed to have visited Kublai Khan. In one French illuminated manuscript of the fourteenth century, Marco Polo is shown having an audience with the Latin Emperor Baldwin in Constantinople and being blessed by the Patriarch of the city before setting out across the Black Sea.

Ibn Battuta was a Moroccan, born in 1304, who travelled as far as India and China and who was received in Constantinople by the Byzantine Emperor Andronicus III Palaeologus in 1332. After the fall of the city to the Ottoman Empire, many in Europe began to look for new sea routes to the East. This process of exploration would lead to many new discoveries in the succeeding centuries. A further consequence of the decline and fall of the Byzantine Empire was that many scholars and academics fled from Constantinople to seek sanctuary in the West, particularly in Italy, and it is thought that this contributed to the start of the Renaissance. This movement of scholars to the West pre-dates the fall of Constantinople and those educated in the city had always enjoyed high international prestige and status because of its impressive academic and artistic legacy.

Many historians, whilst acknowledging the uniqueness of the Byzantine Empire in forming a more or less unbroken link between the ancient world and the medieval period, now regard the fall of Constantinople as marking the end of the Middle Ages. Interestingly, in popular Greek superstition, Tuesday is considered to be the unluckiest weekday because it was the day that the city of Constantinople fell to the Ottoman Empire.

In the centuries following the fall of the Byzantine Empire many western historians came to see it in a generally negative light. Historians writing in the sixteenth century and describing the Eastern Roman Empire were the first to use the term 'Byzantine'.

The word Byzantine has now come to describe any institution, organisation or process that is unnecessarily complicated. Indeed, one dictionary definition makes the term applicable to anything that is 'hierarchical, inflexible; convoluted, complex' (*Cassell Popular English Dictionary*, p 109).

In the eighteenth century, Edward Gibbon wrote in generally disparaging terms of the Byzantine Empire, the decadent and corrupt aspects of its history arguably diminishing an understanding of its achievements and cultural legacy. Whilst corruption and decadence were undeniably major components of the story of the Empire, it is worth remembering that, when much of Europe was in the so-called Dark Ages, Byzantium remained a major centre of education and learning and was the medium through which much knowledge of the Ancient Greek and Roman world was communicated to us today. Steven Runciman, amongst others, has observed that the Western kings and nobles who travelled to the East on Crusade were largely illiterate, ill-educated and ill-mannered in comparison to their Byzantine counterparts who inhabited what was, at the time, the most impressive and cosmopolitan city in Europe. The view of Byzantine culture as being ineffective and self-defeating is likely to have its origins in these encounters. When Byzantine rulers attempted to negotiate with the 'Infidel' they were often seen as traitors to Christendom rather than the experienced, educated and worldly rulers that they were. The jealousy and wonder inspired in the crusaders by the city of Constantinople, where literacy was commonplace and impressive buildings were filled with incredible relics and works of art, is perhaps best demonstrated by the greedy eagerness with which it was seized and sacked during the Fourth Crusade.

By the nineteenth century Byzantium had become almost entirely synonymous with the very worst of human culture. This is exemplified by the opinions of William Lecky who wrote that: 'Of that Byzantine empire, the universal verdict of history is that it constitutes, without a single exception, the most thoroughly base and despicable form that civilization has yet assumed. There has been no other enduring civilization so absolutely destitute of all forms and elements of greatness, and none to which the epithet "mean" may be so emphatically applied... The history of the empire is a monotonous story of the intrigues of priests, eunuchs, and women, of poisonings, of conspiracies, of uniform ingratitude.' (*A History of European Morals from Augustus to Charlemagne*, 2 vols, London 1869, II, 13f).

Arguably, Lecky's pronouncements on Byzantium reveal more about his own mean-spirited prejudices and inadequacies than they do about the city and they also seem rather ironic today, given that the British Empire of which he was a part was to face its own decline and fall in the following century.

In 1928, the Irish poet William Butler Yeats published a collection of poetry called *The Tower* that contained perhaps one of his best-known poems, 'Sailing to Byzantium'. The poem concerns a metaphorical journey made by an elderly man to Byzantium and explores the possibility of finding immortality through the medium of the arts. Byzantium is described as being a holy city and representing a culture that, through its artistic legacy, has achieved an identity unbound by time.

In this symbolic musing on the potential of artistic creation to allow mortal men to escape the essential limitations of their lives, Byzantine culture seems to Yeats to represent an embodiment of this ideal. Within the arena of modern popular culture, and indeed religion and politics, the story of Byzantium continues to fascinate in ways that often deeply divide opinion. The best-selling author of *The Da Vinci Code*, Dan Brown, caused huge controversy with

his questioning of the origins of Christianity and, in particular, with his suggestion, discussed in Chapter One, that
Constantine the Great had invented the divinity of Jesus
Christ turning him from a man into a God through the
medium of the council of Nicaea. Within the world of
popular film also, the spectre of Byzantium emerged in the
cinematic vision of film director Peter Jackson. When
creating and designing the Middle Earth city of Minas Tirith
in his massively popular adaptation of JRR Tolkien's *Lord of
the Rings* trilogy, he apparently based it on medieval
descriptions of Constantinople. Indeed, Tolkien's own
description of the kingdom of Gondor, with its ancient and
noble history of kings threatened by war from the East, is
strongly suggestive of the decline and fall of the Byzantine
Empire.

Perhaps more worryingly Pope Benedict XVI caused an
international furore in September 2006 during a speech to
250,000 pilgrims at an open-air mass close to the German
city of Munich that included a quote from the Byzantine
Emperor Manuel II Palaeologus who ruled from 1391 to
1425. It was taken from a work by the scholar Theodore
Khoury that recounts a conversation about Islam and
Christianity between a Persian and the fourteenth century
Byzantine Emperor. The Pope was quoted as saying, 'The
emperor comes to speak about the issue of jihad, holy
war... He said, I quote, "Show me just what Mohammed
brought that was new, and there you will find things only
evil and inhuman, such as his command to spread by the
sword the faith he preached"', (Daily Mail Online, 17th

October 2006). Although the Pope appeared to avoid offering his own opinion on the statement, many believe that he was courting controversy by its inclusion. Those who defended Benedict pointed out that the Pope was arguing that no religion should attempt to justify the use of violence on the grounds of faith. However, many interpreted his comments as constituting a direct criticism of the Islamic faith. There is arguably a certain irony inherent in the head of the Catholic Church, which historically has had such difficult relations with the Orthodox Church, culminating in the Great Schism of 1054, quoting from a Byzantine Emperor. Even after its fall five and a half centuries ago the Empire still seems to manage to cast a long shadow.

Bibliography

Angold, Michael, *Byzantium*, London: Phoenix Press, 2001

Babinger, Franz, *Mehmed the Conqueror and His Time*, Princeton: Princeton University Press, 1978

Brown, Dan, *The Da Vinci Code*, London: Bantam Press, 2004

Browning, Robert, *The Greek World: Classical, Byzantine and Modern*, London: Thames & Hudson, 1985

Gibbon, Edward, *The History of the Decline and Fall of the Roman Empire*, London: Everyman's Library, 1993

Holland Smith, John, *Constantine the Great*, London: Hamish Hamilton, 1971

Konstam, Angus, *Historical Atlas of the Crusades*, London: Mercury Books, 2004

Mango, Cyril, *Byzantium: The Empire of New Rome*, London: Weidenfeld & Nicolson, 1980

Mayor, Adrienne, *Greek Fire, Poison Arrows & Scorpion Bombs*, London: Duckworth, 2003

Norwich, John Julius, *Byzantium: The Early Centuries*, London: Viking, 1988

Norwich, John Julius, *Byzantium: The Apogee*, London: Viking, 1991

Norwich, John Julius, *Byzantium: The Decline and Fall*,

London: Viking, 1995

Phillips, Jonathan, *The Fourth Crusade and the Sack of Constantinople*, London: Jonathan Cape, 2004

Riley-Smith, Jonathan, *The Atlas of the Crusades*, London: Times Books, 1991

Runciman, Steven, *Byzantine Style and Civilization*, London: Penguin, 1975

Runciman, Steven, *The Fall of Constantinople 1453*, Cambridge: Cambridge University Press, 1965

Wedgwood, Ethel, *The Memoirs of the Lord of Joinville*, Minnesota: Kessinger Publishing, 2004

Web Pages

www.fordham.edu/halsall/byzantium
www.en.wikipedia.org/wik/Byzantium
www.byzantium.ac.uk
www.imperiobizantino.ac.uk
www.newadvent.org/cathen/03096a.htm
www://historymedren.about.com/cs/byzantinestud-
ies/a/forgotten.htm

Index

INDEX